SERIAL COMPOSITION

REGINALD SMITH BRINDLE

SERIAL COMPOSITION

LONDON
OXFORD UNIVERSITY PRESS
NEW YORK   TORONTO

Oxford University Press, Ely House, London W. 1

GLASGOW NEW YORK TORONTO MELBOURNE WELLINGTON
CAPE TOWN SALISBURY IBADAN NAIROBI LUSAKA ADDIS ABABA
BOMBAY CALCUTTA MADRAS KARACHI LAHORE DACCA
KUALA LUMPUR SINGAPORE HONG KONG TOKYO

First published 1966
Reprinted 1967 and 1969

Printed in Great Britain

CONTENTS

ACKNOWLEDGEMENTS

Thanks are due to the following publishers for permission to reprint the musical examples:

Universal Edition (London) Ltd.

Alban Berg. Schliesse mir die Augen beide.
    Lyric Suite.
    Violin Concerto.
    Lied der Lulu.

Arnold Schoenberg. Six Little Piano Pieces. Op. 19.
    Pierrot Lunaire.
    Suite. Op. 25.
    Quintet. Op. 26.
    Third String Quartet. Op. 30.
    Variations for Orchestra. Op. 31.

Anton Webern. Six Bagatelles for String Quartet. Op. 9.
    Zwei Lieder. Op. 19.
    Symphony. Op. 21.
    Three Songs. Op. 23.
    Das Augenlicht. Op. 26.
    Variations for Piano. Op. 27.

Mario Peragallo. Violin Concerto.

Karlheinz Stockhausen. Klavierstücke.
    N° 7. Klavierstücke XI.
    Zyklus for percussion.

Pierre Boulez. Improvisations sur Mallarmé.
    Structures.

Roman Haubenstock-Ramati. Mobile for Shakespeare.

Luciano Berio. Circles.

Bo Nilsson. Reaktionen.

Henri Pousseur. Caractères.

G. Schirmer, Inc., New York.

Arnold Schoenberg. Fourth String Quartet. Op. 37.
    Ode to Napoleon Bonaparte.

Peters Edition.

Arnold Schoenberg. Five Pieces for Orchestra. Op. 16.

Reginald Smith Brindle.　Concerto for Five Instruments and
　　　　　　　　　　　　Percussion.
　　　　　　　　　　Creation Epic.

　　　　　　　　　　Homage to H. G. Wells.

Boosey and Hawkes, London.

Igor Stravinsky.　Canticum Sacrum.
　　　　　　　　Threni.

Edizioni Suvini Zerboni, Milan.

Luigi Dallapiccola.　Il Prigioniero.
　　　　　　　　　　Quaderno Musicale di Annalibera.
　　　　　　　　　　Goethe-Lieder.
　　　　　　　　　　Cinque Canti.
　　　　　　　　　　Canti di Liberazione.

Bruno Maderna.　Serenata N⁰ 2.
　　　　　　　　String Quartet.

Luciano Berio.　Serenata N⁰ 1.

Ars Viva Verlag (Hermann Scherchen) G.m.b.H., Mainz.

Luigi Nono.　Il Canto Sospeso.
　　　　　　　Varianti.

Aldo Bruzzichelli, Florence.

Bruno Bartolozzi.　String Quartet.

　　Thanks are also due to M⁰ Camillo Togni for permission to print
an example from his Ricerca, Op. 36.

To my friend
Luigi Dallapiccola

I. GENERAL

Creative Thought and Compositional Method. Serialism and Free Twelve-note Composition.

CREATIVE THOUGHT AND COMPOSITIONAL METHOD

In composition, our mental activity pursues two separate, but interdependent, lines of thought. One is creative and receives its impulse from fantasy, imagination, and inspiration. The other is occupied with method, with the technical means which give adequate definition to what has been first conceived on the plane of fantasy. Imaginative faculties are naturally a prime necessity for authentic artistic creation, but adequate technical skill is essential if the impulses of creative thought are to be translated into a worthy musical guise. On the other hand, the highest grade of technical ingenuity is of no avail without the fertilizing power of fantasy and inspiration.

Unfortunately there seems to be no universal means of stimulating the imagination and increasing our powers of fantasy. Some have pursued inspiration in exotic and stimulating surroundings, others in tranquillity. Not a few have had recourse to the influence of narcotics, with little conspicuous success. But the truth is that inspiration is a fugitive thing and obeys no man-made laws. Sometimes a man may possess it all his life. More often—and this seems especially the case with composers—inspiration and the urge to create are strong enough in youth, but dwindle rapidly even before the first grey hairs appear. Each of us has his own creative destiny and no amount of tenacity of purpose can change its path, just as no amount of will power can increase our physical stature.

However, there is one way of stimulating creative fantasy which many composers have remarked on, and that is through the very act of working. The most difficult period in a composition is the first conception, but once this has been accomplished, the act of moulding musical material serves as a stimulus to the imagination and creative ideas leap to the mind in profusion. There is plenty of evidence that even great geniuses had to labour hard to bring their first ideas into satisfactory shape, but there is no evidence whatsoever that the same amount of toil had to be expended on creative thought once their compositions got under way. The same is true today and composers who use the serial method observe that, while working, certain note-successions may suddenly reveal latent possibilities, and that the creative faculties of the mind, seizing on these, will form new musical designs. In fact, in serial music, the method itself is a powerful stimulus to the imagination, through the very fact that the creative mind can set to work without delay on already-prepared note-successions. As much serial music features constant change of idea (in contrast to the classical characteristic of relative constancy of idea) it is evident that this close inter-relationship between creative thought and methodical thought is particularly important.

Unfortunately, the workings of the creative mind are so obscure that little more can be said which will be of real assistance. Inspiration and fantasy, such vital elements in composition, are unfortunately elusive and subject to no rule or command. So inevitably our task here is concerned with what can be achieved by methodical thought. We must investigate the expressive potentialities of the basic musical material at our disposal and discuss method—the technical means of achieving valid artistic ends.

Inevitably this book will seem to put exaggerated stress on the importance of method and technique and ignore the great potential values of instinct and fantasy. It must be constantly borne in mind, therefore, that though these latter are rarely mentioned, they are of overriding importance and can drastically alter technical assessments. In fact, method can frequently be found to be at fault, whereas fantasy and intuition are always unerring. According to the estimations of method, there is no reason why Verdi's descending scale melody in the great *La Traviata* aria, or Beethoven's chordal theme in the *Eroica*, should not be just as banal as the same material in the hands of other composers. But these melodies, being born of sublime creative thought, transcend the limitations of their somewhat inconspicuous technical values and reveal these composers in their greatest moments. It must be borne in mind, therefore, that the technical details in this book have no absolute values. A certain melodic note-sequence which theory would condemn, or a chordal progression which is not normally to be recommended may on the contrary, through the force of creative deliberation, prove to be among the most sublime expressions in musical history. A moment of illuminated thought is worth more than a library-full of technical values.

SERIALISM AND FREE TWELVE-NOTE COMPOSITION

The scope of this book is not limited to serial composition. It is also hoped to give an outline of that compositional technique which preceded serialism—the style of 'free atonalism'—and that which is also now emerging from it in the form of 'free twelve-note composition'.

Nevertheless, by far the major part of this book is dedicated to serial composition. The reason is largely one of convenience. For though the style of free atonalism was developed during some fifteen years before serial techniques were formulated and though serialism is now being abandoned by some composers in favour of a free use of the twelve-note 'total-chromatic',[1] serialism contains so many of the compositional principles involved in free writing that it can be regarded as the best discipline a student can undergo in order to have a full command of modern compositional techniques.

Even if a composer's aim is to go beyond serialism into the largely uncharted territory of free twelve-note writing, it is still the best guide along the initial stages of the journey. It is a means to an end and, for the time being, the most effective one.

Discussion of free twelve-note writing is therefore held back until the end of the book, as most of the principles involved will by then be already familiar and conclusions can be drawn with greater facility and brevity.

Only a long time after reading this book will the student finally decide whether his own particular mode of expression is best served by the established technique of serialism or by the self-imposed disciplines of 'free' composition. Perhaps, like some of us, he may prefer to use the best of both worlds. However, it seems that much of the technical detail in this book (e.g. control of tension, interval relationships, twelve-note harmony, formal design, orchestration, etc.) is still valid in many non-serial techniques. These factors are the common property of contemporary musical languages and therefore it is hoped that there is much subject matter in these pages of value to those who reject serial methods and prefer the arduous paths of free invention.

As many who read this book may not have composition as their objective, but may be the more enlightened type of performer or teacher, more involved discussion of compositional factors has been delayed till the latter half of the book. For them the first seven chapters or so may be sufficient, and to assist them as much as possible the early part of the book has been deliberately written in as straightforward and lucid a manner as the subject matter allows.

[1] By 'total-chromatic' I mean all twelve chromatic notes contained in the octave.

2. THE SERIES

General. '*Melodic*' *Series.* '*Tonal*' *Series.* '*Atonal*' *Series. Symmetrical Series. All-interval Series. Symmetrical All-interval Series.* '*Short*' *and* '*Long*' *Series.*

GENERAL

As serial technique is designed to exploit the possibilities of the total-chromatic, it is usual to form a series from a succession of the twelve different notes enclosed within the octave. In this way, none of the twelve notes is omitted, nor is any used twice. Music has been composed with series[1] comprising more and less notes than the conventional twelve, but such usage is abnormal. Certain limitations arise which will be discussed later.

The total number of possible twelve-note series is 479,001,600, but each composer designs the series he uses to suit each individual composition. He does not choose the succession of twelve notes in a purely arbitrary manner, but carefully considers the positioning of every note, weighing its implications and values, so that the series may be perfectly suited in every detail to the music the composer has in mind. What may be an excellent series for one composer may be unsuitable to another. Before going on to the actual method of constructing a series, it will be best to examine various types of series which composers have used, together with the resulting music. In this way, it will be seen that composers have often very different objectives, and therefore the series they use have very varied characteristics.

'MELODIC' SERIES

Arnold Schoenberg has said that 'the first conception of a series always takes place in the form of a thematic character', but qualified this by adding that often the 'first conception' needed to be changed on 'constructional considerations'. This idea of the series as being primarily melodic is by no means universally accepted, but with strongly lyrical composers such as Alban Berg and Luigi Dallapiccola it is obvious that on many occasions the melodic character of the series has been a prime consideration.

Berg's first attempt at completely serial composition was the song 'Schliesse mir die Augen beide' (1925), and in using the same series again

---

[1]Alternative terms for the series are 'tone-row' (U.S.) or 'note-row'. Both are frequently used.

in his next work, the *Lyric Suite* (1926) for string quartet, he seems to confirm that his desire was to use a series with strong lyrical possibilities:[2]

Ex.1   Berg: *Song* and *Lyric Suite*

Though the same notes are used at the beginning of the song and the *Lyric Suite*, it will be seen that the rhythmic configuration used in each case is in considerable contrast, and so creates a complete differentiation between the two melodies:

Ex.2   Berg: *Song*

Schlies - se mir die Au - gen bei-de   mit den lie - - ben

Ex.3   Allegretto giovale (♩ =100)   Berg: *Lyric Suite*
Vln.1
poco *f*

In Dallapiccola's opera *Il Prigioniero* three series are used, each with specific thematic intentions, and melodic fragments of these series permeate the whole work, conveying concepts and hidden meanings very much as Wagner did with his 'leading motif' principles. The main series has an expressive melodic arc, and first appears in definitive melodic form at the words 'O Lord, help me to walk':

Ex.4   come di   Molto lento, ma non trascinato   Dallapiccola: *Il Prigioniero*
lontano   2   3   4   5   6   7   10 11 12
sempre *pp* Si - gno - re,   a - iu - ta-mi a cammi - na - re

This series is therefore associated with prayer, the other two being designated by the composer as the 'series of hope' and the 'series of liberty':

[2]As a series it is not a theme but only a note-sequence, it is usually written out with equal note values.

Ex. 5

"Series of Hope"   Dallapiccola : *Il Prigioniero*

"Series of Liberty"

It will be seen how the 'series of hope' begins with small, tentative melodic movements in chromatic steps, which then gain strength in ever more confident leaps. The melodic shape seems to express a hope which is at first uncertain, but gathers confidence as it reaches full expression. On the other hand, the 'series of liberty' (which can be grouped into three clearly diatonic note-clusters of four notes each) has a bold, confident character, striding onwards without any semitonic hesitancy.

'TONAL' SERIES

First we must define what is meant by 'tonality', in order that later we may appreciate with greater exactitude what is meant by 'atonality'. By 'tonal' music we refer to that music in which a definite sense of key prevails, in which all the notes present are related to a central key note or 'tonic'. A single specific key note may prevail over large musical periods in non-modulating diatonic music. Changes of key centre can be brought about through modulation. But in the case of chromatic harmony, the change from one key centre to another may be quite rapid, even brusque. Yet as long as these key centres are not completely obscured, the music is still regarded as being tonal.

Ernest Krenek, in his excellent treatise on twelve-note composition *Studies in Counterpoint*,[3] recommends us to 'avoid more than two major or minor triads [in the series] formed by a group of three consecutive tones . . . because the tonal implications emanating from the triad are incompatible with the principles of atonality'. This is certainly true, but many of our greatest serial composers have included suggestions of tonality in their works, and some have deliberately courted tonal implications in their music by using series specially designed to permit tonal suggestions with facility. Before considering these deliberately 'tonal' series, let us look again at two of the 'melodic' series already discussed. The series in Berg's song and the *Lyric Suite* (when written out with the flattened notes changed into their enharmonic sharp equivalents) will be seen to embrace definite tonal regions:

[3]G. Schirmer, New York, 1940.

6

Not only does the series contain two minor triads, but the first 'half' of the series (notes 1 to 6) is completely diatonic within the tonality of F major, and the second half (7 to 12) is diatonic within B major. Only one note (the 4th degree, or subdominant, in each case) is lacking from the complete scales of F major and B major in each half of the series.

Similarly, if Dallapiccola's series in Ex. 4 is written out in a slightly altered (but audibly identical) form:

Ex7

it will be seen that the first half of the series comprises a chord of G in both major and minor forms, with the minor 7th and minor 9th. The second half is a 7th chord of F♯ minor, with two auxiliary notes or appoggiaturas (D♯ and B♯).[4]

It will be noticed, however, that the tonal implications here are not as clear as those in Berg's series. Only one triad (G major) is included in three consecutive notes, and elsewhere the tonalities are obscured by auxiliary notes, and minor 7ths and 9ths.

A 'tonal' series, rich in harmonic implications, is that used by Berg in his Violin Concerto (1935). This series, in its original form, is built on alternating minor and major chords for the first nine notes, while notes 9 to 12 form part of a whole-tone scale:

Ex. 8

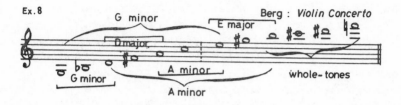

---

[4] B♯ has been used here, rather than C as in Ex. 4, in order to illustrate with greater clarity how the second half of this series forms a chord of F♯ minor with the minor 7th and two appoggiaturas. However, as will be explained in Chapter 3, the use of B♯ (as well as E♯, C♭, and F♭) is usually avoided in serial music.

Clearly, the series moves from the tonal orbit of G minor to that of A minor; in fact the orchestral preparation for the soloist's first exposition of the theme sets out this harmonic structure in great clarity:

However, such a series could tend, by its regular intervallic structure, to produce extreme melodic monotony. It could also be somewhat limited in harmonic resources over a big period, and it is evident that in his Concerto Berg avoided these pitfalls through a serial technique of considerable freedom.

In his *Quaderno Musicale di Annalibera*, Dallapiccola uses a series of more subtle tonal suggestions:

Not only are there three triads present (B major, F major and A minor), but two groups of 3 and 4 notes each comprise notes from the two possible whole-tone scales. These whole-tone groups tend towards a certain harmonic equilibrium within themselves, but not in combination.[5] Further, the first five notes of the series form part of a diatonic area of B major, and the last four that of A minor or F major. It will be seen that this series is much richer in intervals than that of Berg's Concerto, for it

---

[5]There are only two possible whole-tone scales, a semitone apart. As there is no dominant, sub-dominant or leading note in a whole-tone scale, the notes have no tendency to resolve or modulate. No note predominates to produce a feeling of key and therefore music based on whole-tone scales cannot be regarded as tonal. Combinations of notes from the same whole-tone scale are neither completely consonant nor dissonant, but form a pleasant harmonic equilibrium which theory (according to 'natural' laws) has failed to explain satisfactorily. However, note groups from the two scales must not be mixed, if it is desired to maintain the whole-tone harmonic equilibrium.

comprises a semitone, tone, minor third, major third, diminished fifth, perfect fifth, minor sixth, and minor seventh. As the remaining intervals within the octave (fourth, major sixth, and major seventh) could be obtained by inversion of intervals already present in the series, we are dealing here with a series which can therefore produce any interval, and should be rich in melodic possibilities.

In the first piece of the *Quaderno* entitled 'Simbolo', Dallapiccola contrives to reveal the symbol BACH (German nomenclature for B♭, A, C, B♮) in transposed forms beginning as follows:

There is a subtle chromatic movement from B major to A minor here, which is cleverly obscured by the oscillating pedal notes. At first the A♯ functions as a lower appoggiatura to the pedal B, then in bar 3 both notes seem to have a harmonic function. By bar 4 the B has become an appoggiatura to the A♯ (B♭ by now), while in bar 5 neither note forms part of the A minor harmony. It is evident that here Dallapiccola fuses serialism with the functions of chromatic harmony, producing a subtle amalgam of both techniques.

Arnold Schoenberg's series usually demonstrate less evident harmonic tendencies than the 'tonal' series we have so far considered, but his series are usually by no means as non-tonal as one would expect from this 'father' of atonality.

The series of his Wind Quintet Op. 26 is divided into two groups of whole-tones if one considers the 12th note as belonging to group 1 to 5:

9

Schoenberg: *Wind Quintet*, op.26

Though the whole-tone groups would naturally not tend to suggest tonal harmony, they could (as long as notes from the two whole-tone scales are not mixed) produce whole-tone harmony, which is of a mild character, and lacks the virile tensions of atonal note-groupings.

The famous Variations for Orchestra Op. 31, which René Leibovitz has so brilliantly extolled as a paragon of twelve-note technique,[6] is based on a series which not only contains a minor triad and two groups of whole-tone relationships, but in which each four-note group is orientated towards a specific tonality:

Ex.13

Schoenberg: *Variations*, Op.31

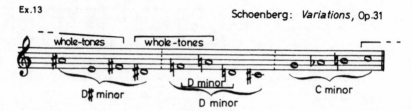

It was not normally Schoenberg's habit, however, to form his series so as to produce tonal suggestions. Only in his *Ode to Napoleon Bonaparte* Op. 41 did he deliberately set out to create tonal associations, and the series for this work is so designed that it is easy to form sixteen different major, minor, and augmented triads:

Ex. 14

Schoenberg : *Ode*, Op. 41

Triad chords derived from each half of series.

[6]In *Introduction a la Musique de Douze Sons* (L'Arche, Paris, 1949).

The harmonic framework of the *Ode* is founded to a considerable extent on these chords, some of which dominate as tonal centres. In fact, the work ends on an unambiguous chord of E♭, and it is generally agreed that this tonality is predominant throughout the whole work:

Schoenberg: *Ode to Napoleon*, Op. 41

Ex. 15

It is obvious, from the 'classical' kind of part-writing, the considerable octave doublings, and agglomerations of triad-formation chords, that in the *Ode* Schoenberg wished to write a work with strong classical associations, while still adhering to a serial form of composition.

'ATONAL' SERIES

'Atonal' music refers to that music which is not clearly organized by traditional systems, such as the modal system, or the major and minor key system. The word 'atonal', meaning 'non-tonal', was at first coined as a derogatory term, equivalent to 'non-music'. 'Atonality' is really a completely mistaken term. For whenever two or more sounds are combined, harmonic relationships are formed. These relationships may be extremely complicated, and outside the realm of traditional harmonic usage, but far from being completely 'non-tonal', they will certainly be formed of an intricate complex of tonal relationships. But the word 'atonality' is by now accepted as signifying an all-inclusive tonality which includes all possible harmonic products of the 'total chromatic space' enclosed by the twelve semitones within the octave.

There is a field of super-tonality which spans the enormous space between diatonic harmony on the one hand, and sheer chaos on the other. This is the field of 'atonality'. Some musicians prefer instead the term 'pantonality', signifying a unification of all tonalities. It seems preferable, but nevertheless is still little used.

Before considering 'atonal' series, we must observe that the all-important factor to be considered is that of atonal equilibrium. There are degrees of atonality which run a path close to that of traditional harmony, but others which are very far indeed from any normal tonal relationships. These various degrees of atonality must not be mixed in haphazard fashion, but must be controlled and graded so that the music either keeps to one atonal field, or maintains an artistic equilibrium between closely related fields, some of which may tend towards lesser degrees of atonality (and therefore moving *towards* tonality), and others towards greater degrees (and therefore moving still further *away* from any tonal suggestions).

The 'atonal' series is therefore, ideally, a series which maintains throughout the same degree of atonality. It is obvious that to do so, all tonal triads must be eliminated, all groups in whole-tone relationship,[7] successions of fourths (which can produce the effect of cadential basses or of harmony based on superimposed fourths) and any group which may form a chromatic chord (such as a diminished seventh chord) which has an obvious traditional feeling.

Therefore an atonal series is usually formed of note-groups of a chromatic nature, such as (in their closest formation) two semitones (①in Example 16), one semitone and a tone ②, one semitone and a minor third ③, one semitone and a major third ④, and one semitone and a fourth ⑤:

Ex.16
'Atonal' note groupings in series.

[7]The objection to whole-tone groups in an 'atonal' series needs some elucidation, for in general they do not contain tonal suggestions (though some groups can form incomplete minor seventh or major ninth chords). The objection is rather that they can form harmony and melody which lack the more virile tensions required in music of a strongly atonal character. However, in serial music of a more euphonious nature, the presence of whole-tone harmonic and melodic fragments can be perfectly admissible, indeed welcome.

Such series are frequently found in Anton Webern's works, for example that used in his Symphony, Op. 21:

Ex.17   Webern : *Symphony*, Op. 21

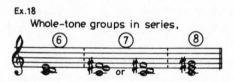

As will be seen, this series contains a preponderance of type ③ note groupings (cf. Ex. 16), of which there are four, and two each of types ①, ② and ⑤.

Webern also used, but to a much lesser extent, groupings of three notes in whole-tone relationship, of which there are only three possible combinations—chords formed from two whole-tones, ⑥ in Ex. 18, one major third and one whole-tone ⑦, and the augmented triad ⑧:

Ex.18
Whole-tone groups in series,

However, when Webern used a series containing whole-tone groups, the chromatic alterations of the notes comprising the group are usually found at a brief distance, thus annulling, to some extent, the effect of whole-tone harmony. This is shown in the series for his Three Songs for Voice and Pianoforte, Op. 23:

Ex.19

Webern: *Songs*, Op.23

It is worthy of comment, too, that in order to preserve the atonal equilibrium in this work, Webern carefully avoided using the group of four notes in whole-tone relationship *in any of the 4-note chords* which are so numerous in the piano part.

SYMMETRICAL SERIES

The series may be formed of two or more portions which are symmetrical in their intervallic structure. It may have been noticed that in the series for Webern's Symphony Op. 21 (Ex. 17) the intervals between notes 1 to 6 are mirrored exactly in reverse (though at a different pitch) by notes 12 to 7. This series is therefore formed of two symmetrical halves, the second in retrograde (12 to 7) being identical with the first half, but transposed a diminished fifth below.

Matyas Seiber, in his *Ulysses*, used a series which shows remarkably symmetrical features:

In the four 3-note groups, Seiber presents three variants of an original group ('O') comprising a rising minor third and a semitone. The variants are inversion ('I'), retrograde ('R') and retrograde of the inversion ('RI').[8] But this is not the only symmetrical feature, for the first six notes are formed from two overlapping 4-note groups (formed from a rising minor third, semitone, and minor third) and the last six notes are formed of the same groupings inverted (i.e. falling minor third, semitone and minor third).

Unfortunately, symmetrical series of this type tend to be somewhat limited in melodic possibilities. The variety of intervals available for melodic purposes is restricted, but not so much as would at first appear. If inversions of intervals are also included (e.g. the minor third may be inverted to become a major sixth) the Seiber series in Ex. 20 offers six different intervals, and the Webern series (Ex. 17) no less than nine out of the eleven possible intervals within the octave. The limiting factor for melodic purposes is that the contour of the series has too little variety, and especially in the Seiber example, skill is needed to avoid melodic monotony. Similarly, the vertical (harmonic) resultants of symmetrical series could tend to lack variety. Care would have to be exercised to avoid the same kind of chords recurring too frequently.

However, the symmetrical series, by its very nature, gives greater unity to a work than a series made up of disparate elements.

ALL-INTERVAL SERIES

Eleven different intervals are possible between the twelve notes of the series, though in reality the five largest intervals (5th, minor 6th, major 6th, minor 7th, and major 7th) are only inversions of the five smallest intervals (4th, major 3rd, minor 3rd, tone, and semitone). The diminished fifth or augmented fourth, being a tritone, does not change on inversion,

---

[8]See Chapter 4 for derived versions of the series.

so only one is present in the all-interval series. There is always a tritone interval, however, between the first and last notes of the series. Though an all-interval series may contain all eleven intervals, in reality it is made up of the five smaller intervals and their inversions, plus one tritone:

Ex.21   Krenek: *Studies in Counterpoint*

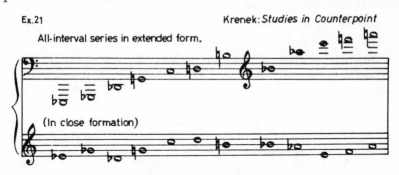

All-interval series in extended form.

(In close formation)

Though this kind of series contains the possibility of maximum intervallic variety, it does not follow that this series is automatically of greatest possible melodic richness. In fact, as excessive variety of intervals tends to dissipate melodic coherence, the all-interval series is not necessarily perfect if melodic qualities are needed. On the other hand, used vertically, it can be a source of more harmonic variety than series built of small symmetrical segments.

SYMMETRICAL ALL-INTERVAL SERIES

The second half of this type of series is symmetrical with the first half, but all intervals in the second half are transposed to their complementary forms, e.g. a semitone becomes a major 7th etc:

Ex.22

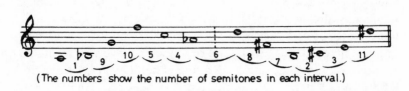

(The numbers show the number of semitones in each interval.)

The second half is therefore a transposed retrograde of the first half. In this kind of series the tritone interval always occurs between notes 6 and 7 and between the first and last notes.[9] Also, it is usual for a triad chord to be found in each half of the series, but not always so, as will be seen from the symmetrical all-interval series used by Luigi Nono in his *Canto Sospeso*:

[9] Cf. also Berg's series in Ex.1

'SHORT' AND 'LONG' SERIES

Some serial works, such as the earlier pieces of Stravinsky's serial period, have been based on 'short' series. For example, *In Memoriam Dylan Thomas* is based entirely on the following chromatic 'cell' of five different notes, and its three possible derived forms[10] (inversion, retrograde, and retrograde of the inversion) and transpositions:

Ex.24   Stravinsky: *In Memoriam Dylan Thomas*

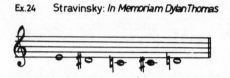

Naturally the use of a short series is in many ways analogous to the practice of forming symmetrical series from variants and transpositions of a small thematic cell. Thus Seiber's series in Ex. 20 is in reality only a three-note series with its derived forms (transposed), and the series to Webern's Symphony (Ex. 17) can be said to be a six-note series with its transposed retrograde.

But there is an important difference between the short series and the symmetrical series made up of variants of a single cell. In the latter, the cell is expanded into a twelve-note series which ranges over the whole total-chromatic. No note is omitted, the atonal equilibrium can be constantly maintained. But with the short series, the total chromatic cannot be used evenly, and inevitably certain notes could dominate and create tonal centres. For instance, if the above Stravinsky series is used in its original, inverted, retrograde, and retrograde of inversion forms, 20 notes are used in all, but we find E used four times, D and D♯ three times, C, C♯, F, and F♯ twice each, and G and A♭ only once. Three notes (A, A♯ and B) are not used at all. If only these four versions of the series were used, the music could tend to polarize around E.

With the short series, the music can therefore only be truly dodecaphonic (i.e. music which exploits continuously the possibilities of the twelve semitones of the chromatic scale) if care is taken to use many transpositions, avoiding the excessive recurrence of any note or notes and the omission of others.

[10]See Chapter 4 for derived forms of the series.

The short series can also have its melodic limitations, and tends (used vertically) to form the same kind of harmonic groupings. On the other hand, the short series can contribute greatly towards the unity of a work, if all detail is formed from the same cell.

'Long' series of more than twelve notes have also been used, usually in cases where composers have felt that the twelve-note series does not yield enough thematic and harmonic variety for an extended composition. This was the case with Schoenberg's String Trio Op. 45, where a supplementary section of six notes is added to the principal twelve-note series. Inevitably, this means that some notes are used twice and others only once during the eighteen-note series. This procedure has been frowned on by some theorists, because it breaks one of the principal laws in serial technique—that no note should recur in a series before all the other eleven have been sounded. However, to all those who consider the artistic quality of music to be immeasurably more important than constructional principles, the series of more than twelve notes is perfectly legitimate and its use amply justified. However, in all but exceptional circumstances such as a work of large proportions in which maximum melodic and harmonic serial possibilities are required, the twelve-note series provides enough material for the most extended composition.

3. CONSTRUCTING THE SERIES

Recommendations for Constructing the Series. Notation. Octave Transpositions.

The foregoing comments on various types of series, each designed with specific ends in view, will perhaps help the student decide which kind of note-succession will best suit his purpose. If he wishes his series to have definite melodic characteristics, or tend to produce certain tonal associations, such factors will be given greatest consideration when constructing the series. The series, in the first case, may be formed from shaping an initial thematic conception. If instead he wishes his music to preserve an atonal balance, and perhaps also have a symmetry which will make for constructional ties and logic, the series will be designed accordingly.

However, our observations on the construction of the series must now be limited to the production of the main type of series—that which maintains an equilibrium of various factors, thematic, harmonic, and constructional—which is used to produce serial music of an atonal character, without traditional melodic and harmonic associations.

RECOMMENDATIONS FOR CONSTRUCTING THE SERIES

1. Avoid melodic progressions which are too traditional in character, e.g. scalic patterns and/or movement in triads.
2. Avoid the use of too many equal intervals, as this could cause melodic monotony.
3. Avoid note-groupings which include major or minor triads, two or more adjacent fourths (cadential basses) or more than three adjacent notes in whole-tone relationship. However, this rule may be relaxed if the notes comprising these 'non-atonal' and whole tone formations are contradicted at a brief distance. Obviously, the 'non-atonal' group which needs most careful liquidation is the major or minor triad.

For instance, in the following series, the B♭ major triad is contradicted by the previous F♯ and the following E and B♮. The whole-tone group B–D♯–A–C♯ is made less conspicuous by the preceding E, and final G♯–C♮:

Ex. 25

4. Avoid note-sequences which belong exclusively to one diatonic scale. For instance, in Ex. 25, the six notes 6 to 11 all belong to the scale of E major.

5. Avoid note-sequences which, in spite of obeying the previous rules, have some hidden cadential quality. For instance, Ex. 25 at first sight seems to have certain possibilities as a series, but when it is played backwards there is a very conspicuous dominant-tonic cadence as E is approached, and E assumes a strong quality as a tonic. This effect is disrupted abruptly by B♭ and F♮ (both very foreign to E major), and then there is a milder dominant-tonic effect on D, F♯, G. This series is therefore unsuitable for writing music which aims at maintaining an atonal equilibrium.

NOTATION

As every altered note may be written as a sharpened form of one note or a flattened version of the next note higher, the use of ♯ or ♭ is often problematical.

The best rule to follow is to use ♯ or ♭ in such a way that firstly, the music looks logical in its horizontal flow, and secondly, vertical note groupings appear in their most conventional forms. In instrumental counterpoint, the horizontal appearance (i.e. as seen in the player's part) takes precedence over the vertical appearance (as seen in the score). Inevitably, it will be necessary that notation follows the pattern set by tonal usage. This seems illogical, in writing atonal music. But if we follow the axiom that the player must be given a part which he can read with the greatest facility, we cannot ignore the need to use accidentals in such a way that they follow the most evident tonal sequences.

For instance, the series in Ex. 25 would appear strange if the notation were as follows:

Ex. 26

whereas in Ex. 25 the accidentals followed the most evident tonal scheme.

The use of C♭, B♯, E♯, and F♭ should be eliminated whenever possible. Firstly, they are never really necessary. Secondly, they do not help the performer. Only sharps and flats should be indicated. ♮ should be eliminated as far as possible, except where it is necessary to cancel an accidental at a close distance, or in the same chord. Some composers use ♮ for every note which is not sharp or flat. This causes an unnecessary proliferation of signs, and the score loses clarity.

If a ♯ or ♭ note is immediately repeated there is no need to repeat the accidental, unless the repetition is carried over into the next bar, or other notes intervene.

OCTAVE TRANSPOSITION OF NOTES IN THE SERIES

The notes of a series can be used in any octave position. As long as the succession of notes is unchanged, each note can be played in any register

4. DERIVED FORMS OF THE SERIES
'O', 'I', 'R' and 'RI' Forms. Transposed Forms of the Series.

The series in its first form is usually called the original, or 'O' form. Some composers, especially American, refer to this as the 'basic set'.

INVERSION

If the first note remains the same, and every interval is inverted (ascending intervals in the original become equivalent descending intervals and *vice versa*) the series is said to be in inverted or 'I' form.

Webern's series for his Opus 23 in its original form:

Ex. 27

from Webern, Op.23

when inverted becomes:

Ex. 28

RETROGRADE

The retrograde form of the series, called 'R', is obtained by reversing 'O' and writing the notes down in the order 12 to 1:

Ex. 29

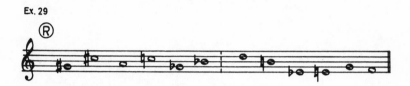

RETROGRADE OF INVERSION

The retrograde of the inversion ('RI') is similarly obtained by writing down 'I' backwards:

Ex.30

'RI' must not be confused, however, with the 'retrograde inverted' form. The latter produces the same succession of intervals as 'RI', but transposed to a different pitch, in this case an augmented fourth higher.

TRANSPOSED FORMS OF THE SERIES

Each series can be transposed so as to begin on any note of the chromatic scale. As well as the original series, there are therefore also eleven transpositions. Similarly, the 'I', 'R', and 'RI' forms can each be transposed eleven times.

Altogether there are therefore forty-eight possible versions of the series. However, with some symmetrical series a transposition of one form of the series may be identical with that of some other form, and naturally forty-eight different patterns are not possible. For example, as the 'R' version of Ex. 17 (the series of Webern's Symphony, Op. 21) is the same as a transposition of 'O' to a diminished fifth below, it is obvious that each transposition of 'R' will be the same as some form of 'O'. Similarly, every transposition of 'RI' will be the same as some form of 'I'. There are therefore only twenty-four possible patterns with this series.

5. WRITING MELODY

(a) Melody of 'Non-traditional' Character.
   1. Interval Relationships. 2. Rhythm in Melody. 3. Silences. 4.
   Formal Design in Melody. 5. Dynamics and Phrasing. 6. Tone
   Colour and Texture. Note Repetition.
(b) Melody of 'Traditional' Character.

A great deal of excellent twelve-note music has been written using melody which retains in varying degrees certain traditional melodic principles. The student can follow the same path, if he wishes to do so. However, it is proposed to demonstrate first the writing of melody which excludes traditional factors, as by so doing the most common serial usages can be illustrated. A short resumé of more traditionally-fashioned twelve-note melody will then follow.

(A) MELODY OF NON-TRADITIONAL CHARACTER

Firstly, it is important to examine in detail all the materials we use in making melody—intervals, rhythms, formal designs, etc.—so that we can become more aware of their potential values. Also it will be seen that what holds good for tonal music is not necessarily valid when working in the atonal field.

1. Interval Relationships

Some intervals have more powerful melodic potential than others. In an atonal context, the larger interval leaps tend to have the greatest emotive suggestion, and are therefore the most powerful melodic factors.[1]

[1] The reason for the greater emotive power of the larger intervals in atonal music needs some explanation. In tonal music, large interval leaps are neither common nor characteristic, but certain examples of their use (e.g. in Elgar's *Enigma Variations* and in Wagner's more chromatic writings) confirm their great power. But on the whole, tonal composers have wrung just as much passion from a semitone as from a major seventh or minor ninth. The reason is that in tonal music, the power of intervals is derived either from harmonic associations or from the particular emotive quality bestowed on each note by its position in the diatonic scale. For instance, the suggestive force of the descending semitone or tone when resolving a suspension is a familiar example of emotive power derived from harmonic stress. The sense of fulfilment when rising from leading note to tonic typifies the emotive quality created in intervals by their position in the diatonic scale.

However, in atonal music, as scalic patterns are completely absent and harmonic associations greatly attenuated, the emotive power of intervals is derived to a considerably lesser extent from these 'exterior' circumstances, and to a much greater extent from a latent 'interior' force within each interval. It is this interior emotive value in intervals that concerns us in atonal music (though it can easily be obscured by external circumstances), and as we have already stated, as a general characteristic large intervals tend to have greater emotive suggestion than small ones. However, this is only a rough generalization and it must be borne in mind that when an interval is too large (say more than a tenth) its emotive value is dissipated. This is because when notes are too far apart, they lose their association with each other and therefore the latent 'interior' power is diminished.

For instance, semitone and tone intervals are melodically weak compared with the minor ninth and major and minor seventh. The thirds are weaker than the sixths. The most stable harmonic intervals, the fourth and fifth, are weakest of all. The tritone interval, having a neutral quality, is usually weak melodically, but in certain harmonic situations can acquire a strong emotive quality. Naturally in atonal music, these 'harmonic' situations will be of rare occurence.

Usually a rising interval is more powerful in emotive content than the same falling interval. Rising intervals are usually assertive and add vigour to the discourse, whereas falling intervals tend towards relaxation and depression. In a rising interval we feel its 'bright' qualities, it is optimistic. But when the same interval is falling, we are aware of its 'dark' side, it is pessimistic.

The following is an approximate scale of intervallic values in melody, the strongest on the left, the weakest on the right:

Ex. 31

However, the relative strength or weakness of an interval is also influenced by its surroundings, by its position in a melodic phrase, by dynamics, and by the rhythmic configuration of which it forms a part. Certain traditional factors can also strengthen an interval's emotive content—if it takes an important part in creating an expressive harmonic effect, if it functions as part of an appoggiatura progression, if it moves on to a strong beat in the bar, and so on. Finally, if the second note in an interval is the highest or lowest of a whole musical section, that interval will probably be endowed with a greater power of suggestion than if it were in a less prominent position.[2]

[2]For those who know Hindemith's *Craft of Musical Composition*, it will be obvious that the scale of melodic values here given in Ex. 31 differs considerably from that of Hindemith. He stresses the major second as being the strongest and most beautiful melodic interval, and refers to it as the chief 'melody builder'. He gives importance to the semitone next, as it can form leading-notes. He also quotes stepwise progression as being the 'ordering principle' of melodic construction. But it must be remembered that Hindemith's conclusions were drawn up only with reference to *tonal* music. In tonal contexts his principles may be excellent, but in the *atonal* field they no longer have the least validity, for the compositional material no longer consists of elements drawn from major and minor scale patterns.

In writing melody, we must be aware that the best results will not necessarily be obtained by always using 'strong' emotive intervals. On the contrary, a succession of strong intervals tends towards incoherence. Strong intervals do not unite easily, and therefore their strength is dissipated. The best melody is usually an amalgam of strong and weak intervals, each placed strategically in its appropriate place. Melody is like speech. It has to have many unimportant words to build up the significance of those that really matter. If speech only consisted of 'strong' words, it would be incomprehensible.

2. Rhythm in Melody

Rhythmic configuration is of extreme importance in twelve-note music.

Traditional melody has as its chief characteristic rhythmic symmetry between the phrases. Often enough, rhythms remain unchanged, or are only slightly varied, over considerable periods. But in all cases the phrase rhythms are related to harmonies, which provide that forward tonal movement which gives complete unity and logic to the progress of the music. As, in atonal music, this tonal forward movement is absent (or at least, is so complex that it has lost much of its power), rhythmic symmetry no longer has validity, and repetitive phrases become trivial and banal.

Also, in traditional melody each note in a phrase contains certain latent harmonic suggestions which endow it with emotive significance in relation to the whole phrase. This latent harmonic suggestion is also comparatively absent in atonal music, and the value of each note in a melody depends not on its harmonic suggestions, but on how that note contributes to the feeling of tension or relaxation required at that particular moment in time.

Rhythms in atonal music must therefore take over part of the function of harmonic suggestion in tonal music. They must propel the music towards points of tension and climax, and also lead the successions of sounds into periods of relaxation and repose.

As a broad generalization, evenly flowing rhythms suggest repose, whereas unequal, jerky rhythms create excitement and agitation. Repose also calls for slow movement and tension for rapid note-successions.

Rhythms in atonal melody are therefore usually asymmetrical and non-repetitive. Phrases often consist of a complex of disparate rhythmic elements.

It is important to note that as rhythm becomes more and more complex and asymmetrical, metre tends to be increasingly obscured, until at a certain point it is completely annulled. It may be there on paper, but audibly the metre has disappeared. This is quite characteristic of much twelve-note music, particularly that in the post-Webern period: in fact metrical obscurity is deliberately cultivated.

3. Silences

Silence has an important place in atonal melody, and in atonal music in general. It can have dramatic effect at points of tension (e.g. the silence at the beginning of bar 8, Ex. 34), and in moments of relaxation can produce the maximum effect of repose (e.g. Ex. 32, the third (silent) bar). Silence is the greatest contrast to rhythmic stress, to harmonic tension, and to rapid movement. It is the most effective means of forming phrases.

4. Formal Design in Melody

Compared with traditional melodic forms, with their symmetrical periods, well-defined and repetitive phrases, and division by cadences into logical tonal progressions and formal periods, atonal melody has a very free, almost improvisatory character. But in the most important factor it must obey the main principle of tonal melody—the music must follow a certain emotional path consistently. It must at first propose an emotive situation, bring it to its climax and then resolve it and round off the story satisfactorily. If the melody is completely 'abstract', it has no emotional development and is therefore sterile. Though atonal melody has often been referred to as 'abstract' or even 'athematic', if it is to be successful it must convey human emotion, even though in the most elusive manner.

The student must therefore give form to his melody by following an over-all design, carefully laid out to express a preconceived emotional plan. The relaxation and tension should be carefully graded. In tranquil music, the degrees of tension will be slight, as in the placid, almost dispassionate piccolo solo (unaccompanied) which begins Bruno Maderna's *Serenata No. 2*:

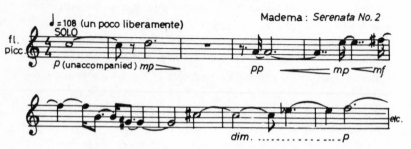

Ex.32

Maderna: *Serenata No. 2*

In dramatic music, they will be forceful:

Ex.33 Berio: *Serenata I*

Sometimes strong contrasts of tension and relaxation will be required, at others the emotion will ebb and flow only gently, so that strong contrasts will be avoided.

5. Dynamics and Phrasing

As the tension and relaxation in atonal melody depends very much on regulation of the 'volume dimension', dynamics should be carefully indicated, so that they contribute to the build-up of a climax, and towards its decline. Phrasings should be carefully worked out, with appropriate legato, staccato, and sforzando indications, designed to reinforce the rhythmic and dynamic designs.

As a rough generalization, tension is produced by staccato phrasing, loud volume, or big dynamic contrasts, relaxation by legato phrasing, soft volume, and small dynamic fluctuations.

We will therefore summarize factors which make for tension and relaxation:

TENSION

Rapid movement
Increasing impetus   }(Time/movement
Strong metrical pulse   dimension)
Irregular rhythms, well defined

Maximum height or depth[3]   }(Pitch dimension)
Strong melodic intervals

Maximum volume
Contrasting silence   }(Volume dimension)
Virile dynamics and strong dynamic contrasts
Staccato phrasing

---

[3]Usually, the highest note in a melody is reserved for the maximum point of climax. However, the lowest note, in quiet dynamics, is frequently used to achieve a point of maximum repose.

RELAXATION

Tranquil movement
Declining impetus
Weak or indeterminate metrical pulse
Flowing rhythms or 'vague' rhythms
} (Time/movement dimension)

Avoidance of extreme registers
Weaker melodic intervals
} (Pitch dimension)

Quiet dynamics
Non-contrasting silence
Less dynamic contrast
Legato phrasing
} (Volume dimension)

Note how relaxation is produced in Maderna's Serenata No. 2 (Ex. 32) by tranquil movement, weak metrical pulse and indefinite rhythms, use of a middle register, the weaker melodic intervals, quiet dynamics, little dynamic contrast and the introduction of non-contrasting silence. There is also a slight increase and decline of impetus. Though no phrasing is indicated, it is obvious that legato is intended. On the contrary, Berio's Serenata I (Ex. 33) is full of dramatic tensions created by rapid movement, irregular rhythms, large compass, strong melodic intervals, big dynamic contrasts, contrasting silences, and the use of staccato, fluttertongue, rapid tremolos, etc. However, Ex. 32 does not contain *all* the factors which create relaxation, nor does Ex. 33 include all those which make for tension, because it is not necessary to use *all* the factors to achieve adequate effects. Music usually consists of combinations of various tension and relaxation effects and there may even be an interplay of contrasting factors. For instance, some elements which tend to create tension, such as rapid movement, may be cancelled out by others which make for relaxation, such as quiet dynamics, flowing rhythms, legato phrasing, etc. It is the *total* effect resulting from the interaction of various factors which has to be considered.

6. Tone Colour and Texture

Tone colour and texture will be given separate consideration later, as they belong more to the field of chamber and orchestral music. But even in the limited region of melody which we are now considering, they are still important. Even if the melody is only for a single instrument, that instrument usually has registers of different colour and intensity, which must be exploited. It is enough to mention the clarinet, with its shrill, tense upper register and rich, virile chalumeau tones, the more relaxed, smooth quality of its upper middle register, and the neutral, 'voicelessness' of the notes just below the 'break'. These can all be turned to fruitful ends.

Texture has little connection with a single-line melody, but it is all-important as a foundation on which to build. It is like the setting for a jewel—unimportant in itself, but of vital importance in creating the whole. This is why texture must be mentioned at this point, though it will only be fully considered later.

The student should first begin by writing short instrumental melodies. He can begin by using simple repetitions of the 'O' version of the series, and then combine the 'O' version with the 'I', 'R', and 'RI' versions. In doing so, it is important to combine the derived forms so that close associations of the same note are avoided. For instance, in the derived forms of the series for Webern's Op. 23 (p. 21) it would be best to follow 'O' with 'I', rather than with 'R' or 'RI', as these latter versions would involve close repetition of notes.

The piece need not necessarily end with the final note of a series.

A theme should not contain phrases which coincide often with the beginning and end of a series. The result would be too mechanical. Phrases should be varied so that they begin and end at different points of the series.

NOTE REPETITION

1. *Notes may be repeated at the same octave pitch, before the next note is played.*
2. *Two notes may alternate in the form of trills, tremolos, and arpeggio effects.*
3. *Complete groups of notes may be repeated, especially when set to different rhythms, before proceeding to the next notes of the series.* Such a procedure often makes for more coherence at the beginning of a theme, and for a greater sense of finality just before its conclusion. However, such usage is by no means common, and many would condemn it as a 'traditionalism'.

In the following example, a short melody for flute illustrates a number of principles outlined in this chapter:

Ex.34

29

The series used is that of Webern's Op. 23 (see p. 21), and 'O' is followed by the derived versions 'I', 'R' and 'RI', in that order. The melody finishes on the sixth note of 'RI', it being considered unnecessary to complete the series.

The melody has been built according to a graph of 'emotive tension values':

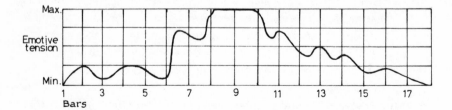

in which emotion begins at a minimum. After two slight surges (bars 1 to 5) it sweeps up to maximum tension (bars 8–9). This is held for a brief spell, and then from bar 10 onwards emotive intensity declines in successive waves back to zero.

It should be noted that:

Maximum tension (bars 8–9) is produced by the highest note (G♯), the most rapid movement (bar 9) and the greatest volume (ff).

Greatest repose (bar 17) is represented by the lowest note (C), the minimum volume (pp) and the minimum movement (⌒).

No rhythm is repeated.

Metrical change is frequent.

In zones of relaxation rhythms flow, are vague, and hide the metrical basis. At the climax rhythms have impetus, are well defined, and strongly confirm the metre (bar 9), but only momentarily.

On four occasions, groups of notes are repeated. The melody thereby acquires greater coherence and eloquence.

Phrasing and dynamics interpret the emotive mood of each note group.

Some valid criticisms of this melody could be made:

(a) The climax is too intense for such a brief piece.

(b) The atonal equilibrium is not maintained towards the end. The last note of bar 12 and the first two of bar 13 form a chord of D minor. This would have been less important if every succeeding note in bars 13 to 16 had not confirmed a D minor tonality. Only the last note of the piece (C natural) contradicts the leading note of D minor, and therefore liquidates this tonal centre. (Naturally this defect could have been avoided by ending with some other form of the series.)

(c) The repetition of note-groups would be strongly disapproved by many composers, as tending to form tonal centres. This is certainly so in bars 13–16. However, the poetic effect of the music is considered to be of greater importance than adherence to 'rules'.

(d) In bar 9, where 'R' follows 'RI', two C♯ notes are in close proximity, but as three notes intervene between them, and the movement is rapid, this has little importance.

(B) MELODY OF 'TRADITIONAL' CHARACTER

As previously mentioned at the beginning of this chapter, much twelve-note music (particularly that of Berg and of Schoenberg's later period) has been written using melodies which deliberately retain traditional characteristics. The principal factor which allies these melodies to tradition is that of rhythm. This can occur in two ways. The rhythm, though mainly non-repetitive, can be sufficiently familiar in type to form immediate traditional associations:

Ex. 35   Berg : *Lied der Lulu*

Wenn sich die Men-schen um mei - net - wil - len um-ge-bracht ha-ben

By using only diatonic notes in C major, the classical shape of the melody becomes still more obvious:

Ex. 36

In Stravinsky's *Canticum Sacrum* the composer makes considerable use of archaic melodic forms. Even the presence of the series does not hide the fact that the origins of the following passage lie in plainsong:

On the other hand, associations with tradition often lie in the use of melodies formed by the repetition and variation of one or more rhythmic cells:

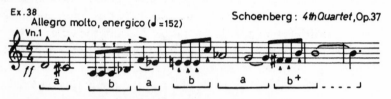

Here the first phrase of the melody is formed by alternations of two rhythms. Rhythm 'a' is varied by diminution in bar 2, and by displacement 'across the bar-line' in bars 3 and 4. Rhythm 'b' is used twice without variation, but in bar 4 begins off the beat, and its last note is prolonged. Also worthy of note is the fact that the notes in 'a' always descend, and those in 'b' always rise.

The above melody therefore demonstrates a very logical and economical form of construction. However its origins are unquestionably classical. Beethoven used this form of cell construction to a considerable extent.

If the series of Ex. 38 is replaced by diatonic notes, the classical nature of the melody lies revealed in a particularly banal form:

To illustrate further the importance of rhythmic configuration in twelve-note music, we will make an experiment in the opposite direction. Now we will rewrite a theme (based on two rhythmic cells) from a Mozart piano sonata:

using the series from Schoenberg's Op. 37 (Ex. 38):

Ex.41

Though what was originally diatonic in Mozart has now become chromatic, the music remains essentially classical in outline, and with appropriate harmonies could resemble the music of Brahms.

From this discussion we can therefore draw a definite conclusion:

If a melody is written with traditional rhythmic configurations, it tends to retain its traditional character, even when the note-patterns are derived from the series.

This statement is also valid for other factors—contrapuntal figurations, accompanimental designs, etc.

This brings us to two fairly valid generalizations:

In classical music the rhythmic patterns remain constant. Diversity is achieved by using different notes:

Ex.42   Beethoven : *5th Symphony*

Allegro con brio

Here it is the rhythms which give complete identity to the music, while the actual notes used contribute considerably less to the music's uniqueness.

In serial music it is the notes which remain the same (i.e. the series). Diversity is achieved by using different rhythms.

In serial music, it is the series which gives identity and unity to the music. Rhythmic configuration cannot do so, as it is always changing.

However, these generalizations must not be taken as an absolute prohibition against the use of traditional elements in serial music. It is all a question of degree. Many composers have made use of classical rhythmic configurations in serial music. But not always in an over-obvious way. The traditional elements are usually sufficiently masked by non-traditional figurations, so that the music ceases to retain an excessively classical identity. Indeed the presence of atonality is often sufficient in itself to give an adequate feeling of contemporaneity to music which in most other detail is quite traditional. Berg's music, for instance, is very largely built on traditional rhythmic designs, yet its atonal basis allowed the music to be a very potent vehicle of expressionist thought.

Therefore, if a student wishes, he can write serial music using a discreet proportion of traditional rhythmic patterns. As at present we are only dealing with melody, it is sufficient to say that traditional melody should be studied in books dedicated to that purpose. Here such matters are out of place, and cannot be dealt with at sufficient length. Nor does this writer pretend to be an authority on such a subject.

After a grounding in the writing of traditional melody, the student can then turn to adapting these principles to serial writing. Later he may go on to fuse these traditional ideas with the 'non-traditional' principles laid out earlier in this chapter. But in the serialization of classical melodic shapes, many factors will cause trouble. The absence of tonal cadences (the magnetic poles of melodic phrases), of forward harmonic movement, of latent harmonic values in melodic notes—all these will tend to turn his melodic shapes into negative statements, until the student has taught himself many of the secrets of this 'middle course' language which must be learned by intuition. This is difficult terrain, where the only genuine way of instruction is for the student to teach himself, by trial and error, as others have done before him.

It only remains, in this section dealing with melody, to recommend the student to discover the melodic medium which best suits his own talents. Between the traditional-type melody and non-traditional there is an enormous field which he can explore. He can either abandon tradition, or use it as a subtle ally to create his own personal form of expression. If he so wishes, he need not write melody at all! Some excellent music has no vestige of what would ordinarily pass for melody. The important thing is for the student to do, with conviction, what he feels to be necessary for his complete self-expression. Such a procedure will be of more value, to him and to others, than his blindfold imitation of any prevailing fashion of the moment, which today may be new, but tomorrow already tarnished and outdated. If he does not write as his own ideals dictate, he does himself a grave disservice, and his music will neither ring true, nor be of any great significance.

6. WRITING IN TWO PARTS

Consonance, Dissonance, and Tension of Intervals. Control of Tension.
The Importance of Register. Avoiding Octaves and 'False Relations' of
the Octave. Melody and Accompaniment in Two Parts. Two Independent
Voices (One Predominating). Two Independent Voices of Equal Importance.
Contrapuntal Forms in Two Parts. Repeated Notes.

Before beginning to write music in two parts, consideration must be given
to the vertical or 'harmonic' aspect of intervals. Some intervals are consonant, other dissonant. Each has its own individual significance, and successions of intervals must be so managed that musical reason is satisfied. In
tonal music, this is done through well defined harmonic principles. But in
twelve-note music, other criteria are used. Our concern is now to control
the degrees of tension in interval-successions, so that an atonal equilibrium
may be maintained, with a satisfactory flow of tension towards climaxes,
and of relaxation towards points of repose.

Some twelve-note music (as will be seen later) can be analysed according
to tonal principles, and it is evident that some composers use traditional
harmonic criteria to some extent in writing serial music. But to compose
with the material of two separate systems, constantly reconciling one with
the other, is a highly skilled operation, aimed at producing a personal
idiom which bridges the gap between the tonal and atonal worlds.

For the moment, we must consider composition only according to
purely serial methods. Our main concern here is with atonal music, so we
must consider the nature of intervals according to atonal criteria, and not
according to traditional harmonic principles.

CONSONANCE, DISSONANCE, AND TENSION OF INTERVALS

Intervals are of two types—consonant and dissonant. But the *degree* of
consonance or dissonance varies in each case. First we will consider the
consonances, which are seven in number:

Ex.43

They have been arranged in order according to their degrees of consonance, the strongest interval (the unison) on the left, the weakest (the

major sixth) on the right. It will be noticed that there is no octave, as this interval is usually eliminated in twelve-note music (see p. 40).

It will be noticed that this group of consonances (apart from the unison) consists of only three intervals (fifth, major third, and minor third) and their inversions (fourth, minor sixth, and major sixth). The inversions are regarded as being less consonant than the original interval. This is particularly so as regards the fourth. Whereas the fifth is completely stable harmonically, the fourth can be somewhat unstable. After a succession of dissonances the fourth appears as a stable consonance:

Ex.44

but after a succession of consonant intervals, the fourth can be less stable, having a 'cadential' tendency for the upper note to resolve downwards:

Ex.45

In atonal music, this cadential quality of the fourth should be carefully avoided.

There are five dissonant intervals, but as one of them, the tritone, can in certain situations assume a consonant character, we will deal first with the four unambiguously dissonant intervals:

Ex.46

The minor seventh is not as dissonant as the major second. In turn, these dissonances are mild in comparison with the harsh dissonance of the major seventh, and the still harsher minor second. Again, it will be noticed that these dissonances really comprise only two intervals (the major and minor second) and their inversions. The inversions are less dissonant than the original intervals.

The fifth dissonant interval, the tritone, is frequently termed a 'neutral' interval. On its own it has the effect of a mild dissonance:

but in successions of whole-tone intervals, it can appear fairly consonant:

Ex.48

After a succession of harsh dissonances, the tritone appears quite consonant:

Ex. 49

but after a succession of consonances it assumes a more dissonant quality:

Ex.50

So far, we have considered only the consonance and dissonance of intervals. But as in atonal composition our main concern is with their degree of tension, we will now establish the scale of tensions in all intervals, observing that the degree of tension is in proportion to that of dissonance:

Ex. 51

The degree of tension is weakest in the most consonant intervals (unison, fifth, and fourth) and increases slightly with the less consonant thirds and sixths. Tension increases rapidly with the mildly dissonant minor seventh and major second, and climbs to its maximum through the major seventh to the minor second. The tritone is of variable tension according to its situation as a consonance or dissonance.

These various degrees of tension are the bricks and mortar of atonal music, they must be carefully graded, to maintain an atonal equilibrium. Tensions must be accumulated to form climaxes, and dissipated to produce zones of repose.

This principle is easily applied in the style of 'free atonalism' (i.e. the creation of atonal music without using serial principles). But using the series, where the note-successions are predetermined (by the series), the control of tension successions becomes difficult. Lack of control, by regarding the series as 'infallible' and blindly writing down note-combinations as the series dictates, can result in those ugly associations of consonance and excessive dissonance which are inelegant, and jar on our sensibility.

As an illustration of the means of controlling tension, let us form a succession of intervals from the series of Webern's Op. 23 (Ex. 27). We will combine notes in the 'O' version as follows:

$$12 \cdot 11 \cdot 10 \cdot 9 \cdot 8 \cdot 7$$
$$1 \cdot 2 \cdot 3 \cdot 4 \cdot 5 \cdot 6$$

This conforms with the combined first six notes of the 'O' and 'R' versions:

Ex.52

The result is a succession of consonances except for the tritone (11 and 2) which introduces a mild dissonance. This passage has little tension therefore, and such interval relationships would be ideal for a zone of repose.

But what if a zone of increasing tension is needed? The notes would have to be manipulated so as to bring into apposition intervals which move towards greater tension:

Ex.53

Though the same notes are used as in Ex. 52, the result is quite different. After beginning with only mild tension (12 and 1) the music moves into a field of intervallic stress, ending on a degree of acute tension. Whenever consonances occur (10 and 3, 4 and 9, 5 and 6) they are always unstressed and passed over quickly. They are not allowed to become prominent.

However, in order to turn the music into a channel of tension, some manipulation has been resorted to. For instance, the lower voice consists now of notes 1.2.3.4.8.5. The upper voice is similarly altered. But *such alterations are legitimate if warranted by the aesthetic result.* To deny such liberty would be mere pedantry.

On the other hand, supposing a serial arrangement of notes formed a tense and discordant succession of sounds, such as:

Ex.54

This could be turned by manipulation into an almost completely relaxed passage:

Ex.55

Naturally, this kind of manipulation is easy as long as the time values of the notes are free. But if they are already determined (as in canons) the operation becomes much more difficult. Nevertheless, it is always possible to arrange sounds as we wish, and not as the series dictates, and we should always be sure that this is exactly what is happening, and not *vice versa.* Otherwise the result will be distorted and inelegant.

THE IMPORTANCE OF REGISTER

So far, we have only considered intervals within the octave. The situation changes considerably when intervals are transposed into different registers. If the notes of a dissonant interval are placed more than an octave apart, the tension is reduced.

Thus the minor ninth is much less tense than the semitone:

Ex.56

But if the distance between the C and D♭ is increased even more, the interval loses its dissonant quality to such an extent that it seems almost consonant:

Ex.57

Similarly, the varying degrees of consonance are less perceptible when the notes are far apart.

We can therefore conclude that *the varying degrees of tension between notes comprising the various intervals become more uniform in proportion to the distance separating the notes.*

The register of each note is therefore of considerable importance in determining the degree of tension or relaxation it can contribute at any given moment.

Naturally, a great deal of the preceding remarks about intervallic tension and the importance of register is also valid, not only for two–part writing, but for music in any number of parts.

AVOIDING OCTAVES AND 'FALSE RELATIONS' OF THE OCTAVE

1. *The interval of the octave should be avoided.* In part–writing it brings one note into undue prominence. This emphasis of a note by octave doubling may cause it to stand out as a tonal centre, thus disturbing the atonal equilibrium. Furthermore, the presence of an octave in a succession of intervals or chords will produce an undesirable void in the tension flow; in fact this *weakening* effect of the octave is more serious than its tendency to form a tonal gravitation. (Very occasionally, however, passages in octaves are used as a colouristic effect. Though there are no really valid objections to this atmospheric device, it is very seldom used in twelve–note music.)[1]

2. False relations of the octave are also to be avoided, as they have the same effect as the octave, but to a lesser degree. *A note emitted by one voice should not be sounded by another voice in a different register before the first voice has passed on to a different sound:*

false relation   false relation
of the octave.   avoided.

[1]Some serial works contain octave doubling throughout extended passages, but this occurs in instrumental writing which follows the classical usage of doubling parts in octaves so as to thicken the texture. Invariably, this procedure occurs in music of a more traditional character (cf. Ex. 15) and is never found in post-Schoenberg works.

In music of more than two parts, false relations of the octave between the *outer* parts are naturally more serious than between inner parts.

1. Melody and accompaniment in two parts

The most simple form of two-part writing is that in which one part predominates as a melody, and the other provides a simple background accompaniment. Such an example is found in the fourth piece (*Linee*) of Dallapiccola's *Quaderno Musicale di Annalibera*:

Ex.59   Dallapiccola : *Quaderno*

Here, the accompaniment (right hand) forms an undulating 'harmonic' background using the 'O' version beginning on A♮. The seventh note (G♭) is omitted but begins the next phrase of melody. The theme (left hand) here uses the 'I' version beginning on A♭.

This short piece (it only lasts 40 seconds) is then completed by transferring the melody to the right hand (notes 7, 11, 10 and 12 of 'O'), and the accompaniment to the left hand (notes 5, 6, 8, 9, 7, 11, 10, and 12 of 'I').

Both hands therefore use all twelve notes of the 'O' and 'I' versions, but in the second half of each version the note order is changed to a considerable extent, though it will be seen that the note-order in each version is changed in exactly the same way. Evidently the composer decided to depart from the normal ordering of the series so as to improve the musical result. Indeed it will be found that the use of notes 7 and 8 (G♭ and C) in the right hand in bar 4 is not as satisfactory as notes 8 and 9. This freedom in serial usage is always completely justified if an improved artistic result is thereby obtained. Otherwise, of course, it is pointless.

The Gavotte of Schoenberg's Suite for Piano Op. 25 is slightly more complex, and contains an accompaniment which has much more definition through imitation of rhythms in the melody:

The rhythm 'A¹' (bar 2, right hand) is reproduced in the left hand (A²) in bar 4. The intervals, however, are not reproduced. This is called 'rhythmic imitation'.

Similarly rhythm 'B¹' (bar 3) in the right hand is reproduced in the left hand at B² in bar 4. The first note is prolonged. Again, this is rhythmic imitation, without strict imitation of intervals.

The use of the series demonstrates interesting points. The right hand part contains notes 1 to 8 of the 'O' version, and then notes 1 to 8 of a transposed 'I' version. The left-hand part is confined to the remaining four notes of these 'O' and 'I' versions, used in each case in the order 9, 10, 11, 12, 11, 10, 9. Naturally, with this kind of serial usage, octaves and false relations of the octave can hardly occur.

2. *Two independent voices (one predominating)*

The Wind Quintet Op. 26 of Schoenberg contains a section in which a horn melody predominates, with an independent countermelody for bassoon:

Ex. 61 Andante   Schoenberg: *Quintet*, Op.26

The use of the series here is interesting. The two parts are derived from the 'O' form of the series (see Ex. 12) in such a way that the same succession of twelve notes, though divided between the two instruments, constantly recurs. But in each of the three appearances of the series, Schoenberg has so contrived the note-distributions that the horn only plays four notes and the bassoon the remaining eight. Furthermore, each of the three four-note groups played by the horn contains different notes, so that, in all, the whole of the series is used.

The horn's four-note groups are arranged as follows:

$$1 \cdot 6 \cdot 7 \cdot 12$$
$$2 \cdot 5 \cdot 8 \cdot 11$$
$$3 \cdot 4 \cdot 9 \cdot 10$$

The symmetrical nature of these groupings will be easily seen.

Similarly, the bassoon part consists of three symmetrically ordered groups of eight notes:

$$2 \cdot 3 \cdot 4 \cdot 5 \cdot \quad 8 \cdot 9 \cdot 10 \cdot 11$$
$$1 \cdot 3 \cdot 4 \cdot 6 \cdot \quad 7 \cdot 9 \cdot 10 \cdot 12$$
$$1 \cdot 2 \cdot 5 \cdot 6 \cdot \quad 7 \cdot 8 \cdot 11 \cdot 12$$

which naturally comprise the twelve notes twice over.

43

This method of dividing the notes of a series between two (or more) parts in a *horizontal-vertical disposition*, so that the whole twelve notes regularly recur, is an excellent one, with two strong advantages:

1. *Octaves or false relations of the octave cannot occur.*
2. *Though the twelve notes recur regularly, they are divided between the parts in such a way that* horizontally, *each thread of the music can be made up of constantly varied note-successions.* Through a maximum unity (the recurrence of the one series) *can therefore be obtained a maximum variety* (in each horizontal part).

Schoenberg's use of this serial method, with his symmetrical note groupings, is here extremely rigorous. But the symmetry, though at first sight logical, and having a certain intellectual appeal, can have little *audible* value. On the contrary, once we are aware of the nature of the serial organization, this music sounds more than ever inflexible and square.

But if we preserve freedom in the application of this *horizontal-vertical* method of distributing the twelve notes between the parts, this practice can be strongly recommended as being both simple, and producing excellent results.

3. Two independent voices of equal importance

Two parts are seldom completely equal in importance except in canonic or other contrapuntal structures, or where they both combine to give a single complete discourse. We are here only concerned with this latter instance.

In the first bar of *Klavierstucke* (1954) by Karlheinz Stockhausen there are two parts of equal importance, and though one part has no thematic relationship with the other, both are equally necessary for the completeness of the music:

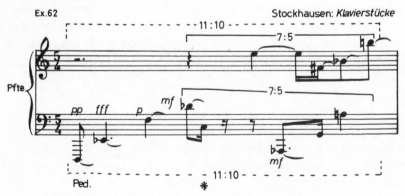

Ex.62   Stockhausen: *Klavierstücke*

Though at two points both parts sound exactly together, neither part is subservient to the other.

In Ex. 62 we can observe two factors of considerable importance—
(1) the extreme irregularity of rhythmic configurations, and (2) the complete
liquidation of audibly perceptible metre. Compare now with the Schoenberg examples, Exx. 60 and 61, which will be seen to be based on completely traditional rhythmic designs.

4. Contrapuntal forms in two parts

Contrapuntal forms (especially canon) are frequently used in serial
music. There are three principal reasons:

Firstly, the note-successions of the series are most naturally disposed in
horizontally flowing streams.

Secondly, contrapuntal forms contribute to the audible coherence of
twelve-note music as long as the form of counterpoint is easily discernable, e.g. a simple canon, not in inverted or retrograde form.
However, if the contrapuntal form is obscure (e.g. a retrograde canon
by inversion), the coherence is lost and the music becomes enigmatic.
But some composers deliberately cultivate this enigmatic quality, and
such canons are an easy road to this end.

Thirdly, counterpoint is one of the few conventional formal devices
which give definite shape to music, without incurring tonal obliga-
tions. Contrapuntal procedures have therefore been much favoured by
serial composers, because they give music a highly organized form,
without involving the composer too much with problems of tonality.

This is probably why Schoenberg chose to write the Trio of the Minuet
of his Suite for Piano Op. 25 as a canon by inversion in two parts:

Ex. 63   Schoenberg: *Suite,* Op. 25

Thus, what is usually a whimsical, genial musical episode, has here become a rather abstruse academic exercise. The square regularity of the rhythms produces music of stolid seriousness, lacking in that subtlety, nuance, and fantasy which we expect with this musical form.

Again to be noted is Schoenberg's symmetrical use of the series. The left hand uses 'O' and 'I' versions of the series beginning on E, the right hand the 'I' and 'O' versions beginning on B♭. In all cases the musical phrase consists of twelve notes, and is divided into two sub-phrases of six notes each.

Dallapiccola is to be noted for his ability to write elegant, lyrical music through the medium of canon. He is able to dominate the straight-laced, 'academic' air of canonic structures, and make them breathe out that delicate, poetic atmosphere which permeates so much of his music. A typical example is the second piece of his *Goethe-Lieder:*

Here the voice part consists of two main sections, one being the retrograde of the other. From half-way in bar 9, the voice part is 'mirrored',
and returns to the beginning. Slight changes are made, but only to accom-
modate the words. At bar 8, the E♭ clarinet joins in, playing the vocal
part forwards, while the voice sings the same part backwards. This is
canon by retrograde motion. The only changes made are in the dynamics.
Only 'O' and 'I' versions of the series are used, the 'I' version being
transposed up a semitone.

The rhythmic patterns of this example are worth noting. The lyrical
quality of the music owes much to the flexible rhythms used. Note-values
are constantly changing, each note-group is made up of different components, and in the whole of the voice part, *no rhythm is ever repeated*.
Classical rhythmic patterning based on the repetition of clearly defined
'cells' are therefore avoided, and this is the principal factor which contributes to the almost intangible lyrical quality of the music (as opposed
to the well-defined lyricism of classical music).

REPEATED NOTES

Before concluding this chapter on two-part writing, we must note the
general practice observed when notes are repeated in polyphonic writing.
The example quoted from Schoenberg's Wind Quintet (Ex. 61) shows
four instances of note repetition, divided into two classes:
1. notes repeated in one part while the other part does not move, e.g.
bar 6 to 7 (horn repeats E).

2. repetition of a note in one voice, while the other moves to one or more other notes, e.g. bars 2, 3, and 4.

We can therefore establish two axioms:

(a) *Repetition of a note can occur while other notes of the series are sustained.*

(b) *Repetition of a note can occur after the emission of other notes which follow it in serial order, as repeated notes can be considered to be single sustained sounds.*

7. MUSIC IN SEVERAL PARTS AND SERIAL USAGE

Music in Several Parts. Serial Usage. The Horizontal-vertical Method. Segmentation. Contemporaneous Use of Different Versions of the Series. Common Thematic Shapes. Expansion into Numerous Parts. Schoenberg's Series. Comments on Serial Manipulation.

MUSIC IN SEVERAL PARTS

After our study of music in two parts, it would be logical enough to continue with the time-honoured academic approach of chapters on three-part writing, four-part writing, and so on. But in serial music, a constantly fluctuating number of parts is such an essential feature, that we will deliberately avoid an extended discussion of three- and four-part writing, limiting our observations to aspects of serial usage and leaving the essential factors of polyphony and harmony until later chapters on these subjects. Another valid reason for not insisting on three- and four-part studies is that they are liable to create habits and inhibitions. How many student compositions in conventional music are in four parts because of habit, or because of the ingrained inhibition that music must be in four parts to be complete? At all costs, such habits and inhibitions must be eradicated by the formation of a contrary practice—that of using just the right number of sounds (many or few) required at any given moment to fulfil expressive needs. As an example of this flexibility as to the number of parts in serial music, we quote a few bars of the accompaniment from Webern's *Zwei Lieder*, Op. 19, for choir and five instruments:

49

As will be seen in this short excerpt, there are not only single sounds, but simultaneous combinations of two, four, five, and seven notes. Both upper and lower staves contain elements of both single-voice melodic phrases and chordal patterns which resolve into a less complex musical design than at first appears. This would be more evident if details of the orchestration were given, but these have been deliberately omitted in order to illustrate that fluctuating density of note-groupings which is such an essential feature of much serial music.

SERIAL USAGE

In discussing various ways of using the series, we will make use of parts based on the following three different rhythms:[1]

Each way of using the series will produce different musical results, some will be satisfactory, others will have to be modified in order to produce good effect, but we will reserve full comment on this till later. Eventually it will be shown how the same three rhythms can be expanded into music of many and varying numbers of parts like the Webern example just quoted.

In all cases the series used will be that of Webern's Songs, Opus 23, as shown in Exx. 27–30.

THE HORIZONTAL-VERTICAL METHOD

One of the most simple and efficient ways of using the series is to let the serial note-order follow the occurrence of each note in time. That is, the series follows a horizontal path (from left to right) but also a vertical one (up and down), tracing a route which follows the beginning of each new note, no matter in which part it may occur. Applying the 'O' version of Webern's series (Ex. 27) to the three rhythms chosen, the result is as follows:

---

[1] These rhythms have been chosen quite arbitrarily. They could form music based either on rhythmic cell constructions (which will be discussed later) or music of a freely contrapuntal nature.

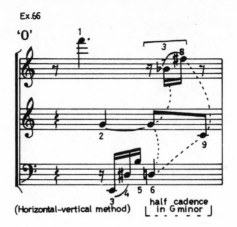

Ex.66

(Horizontal-vertical method)

half cadence
in G minor

According to the nature of the three rhythms, the upper part begins first (note 1) followed by the middle part (note 2). The lower part then enters with four consecutive sounds (notes 3 to 6), followed by the upper part (notes 7 and 8) and the section is completed by the middle voice (note 9). Naturally, sounds have been transposed in register in order to produce a satisfactory musical effect.

This example immediately reveals defective results which are frequent enough in all kinds of serial usage, defects consisting mostly of octaves, false relations of the octave, unwanted tonal note-groups and note-combinations which produce a poor tension-flow (see Chapter 8 on Twelve-note Harmony). In this example the notes comprising the first two beats (notes 1 to 5) form the chord of E minor with major seventh and minor ninth. However, the effect is not excessively tonal as the prominent dissonance (F–G) between the upper parts claims our attention, while the characteristic E minor notes (E and B) are rapidly passed over in the bass. This note-group is therefore not prominently tonal and can be regarded as satisfactory in a mildly atonal scheme.

However, the final beat comprises a completely obvious half-cadence in G minor. Though on paper the F♯ in the upper part ceases before the C in the middle voice begins, in practice the F♯ sounds on in our minds, so that notes 6, 9, and 8 conclude the bar as a seventh chord on D, following a second inversion of the chord of G minor. Naturally, there would be nothing wrong in such a half-cadence if it had been carefully arranged as a desirable musical event, but as it has occurred in a purely fortuitous way in a context where an atonal norm has been aimed at, we can only regard it as technically and aesthetically undesirable. In an atonal context, the effect would be catastrophic. The only way to avoid this half-cadence is by *serial manipulation*, that is, re-ordering the note successions so that suitable note-combinations occur.

By serial manipulation, this example can be re-written as follows:

Ex.67

(Ex.66 rewritten)

The third beat now contains no obvious tonal relationships and the presence of two successive tritone intervals (G–C♯ and G♯–D) is a good feature, producing that vagueness of harmonic effect characteristic of twelve-note harmony in a mild degree of tension.

It will be noticed, however, that whereas our first example used notes 1 to 9 of the 'O' version, this second solution introduces notes 10 to 12 in retrograde and omits notes 7, 8, and 9. Though it would have been ideal to use only the original nine notes, frequent attempts to do so without considerable manipulation proved less satisfactory than the solution adopted. Naturally, in a continuation of this music, notes 7 to 9 would be used next in order to complete the use of the whole series before beginning again with the 'O' or some other version.

In this 'horizontal-vertical' method, it is possible to write extended pieces without using many derived forms or transpositions of the series. This is because the note-order in each horizontal part is constantly changing and because vertical combinations of notes are seldom repeated. Some composers, in using this method, form a 'chain' of several versions of a series. For instance, a 'chain' of 47 notes can be formed by joining together the 'O', 'RI', 'R', and 'I' versions in examples 27 to 30. This chain of 47 notes could be repeated again and again without any monotony of note-order occurring in a piece of moderate proportions.

SEGMENTATION

In segmentation, the series is divided into various segments and these allotted to each part. For instance, in the following example notes 1 to 4 of the 'O' version are given to the lower part, notes 5 to 8 to the middle voice and notes 9 to 12 to the upper part. As the middle voice comprises only two notes and the upper part only three, it is obvious that these parts will continue with the notes 7, 8, and 12 as shown in parentheses:

Ex.68

(Segmentation)

C major   B major-minor

Again the result is not very satisfactory. The first two beats are too obviously centred on C major, moving on the third beat to a group in B major (with seventh, ninth, and minor third). The close spacing of notes in the bass—a poor feature—has been deliberately adopted to emphasize this tonal movement. Again, serial manipulation has to be resorted to in order to establish more 'atonal' note relationships:

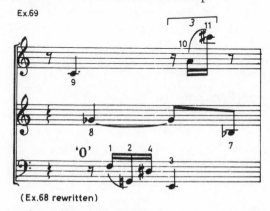

Ex.69

(Ex.68 rewritten)

It will be seen that while the upper part remains unchanged, note-orders in the middle and lower voices have been altered and particularly through tritone intervals (C–G♭ and E–B♭) a mild degree of atonality is preserved throughout the example. Compare the more satisfactory and powerful effect of the widely-leaping bass with the closely-spaced bass movement in the previous example.

SIMULTANEOUS USE OF DIFFERENT VERSIONS OF THE SERIES

In the following example the 'R', 'RI', and 'I' versions (Exx. 29, 30, and 28) are each allotted to a separate voice. However, in the middle voice, the last note cannot be A (2 of 'RI') because this would cause false relations of the octave with the A which has just been sounded in the upper part. Furthermore, a chord of A seventh would be created on the last quaver of the bar. Nor can C♯ (3 of 'RI') be used for the same reason.[2] It has therefore been necessary to use B♭ (4 of 'RI') to avoid these defects:

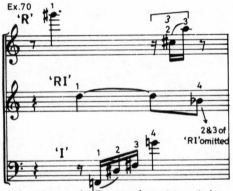

(combination of different versions of the series)

Another undesirable feature is that the bass, after leaping in a decisive manner to the high G, forms a strong consonance (and therefore a weak effect) with D in the middle part. However, as the effect of this perfect fifth is immediately obliterated by the C♯–A in the upper part, there is some justification for refraining from further serial manipulation.

TRANSPOSITIONS

Composers very frequently transpose all versions of the series in order to avoid the monotony of the same note-successions recurring too frequently. As we already know, forty-eight forms of the series are possible through transposition, and sometimes composers use all these possibilities in an extended composition. However, the use of many transpositions is by no means necessary and with a little ingenuity in serial usage it is possible

---

[2]Though the upper part is silent on the last quaver of the bar, the last note sounded (A) continues to sound on in our minds and therefore must not be ignored when considering the effect of note combinations on the last quaver.

to write at considerable length with a minimum of transposition.

In the following example, while the 'O' version at original pitch is used in the upper part, the lower parts are formed from a horizontal-vertical use of 'R' transposed to a diminished fifth below:

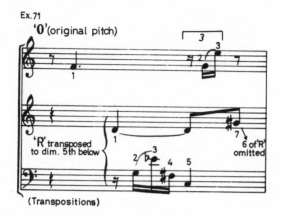

Again some alteration is necessary. If E (6 of 'R' transposed) is used as the last note of the middle part, false relations of the octave will occur with the E in the upper part. Also a chord of C major will be strongly evident. This E has therefore been replaced by G♯ (7 of 'R' transposed).

COMMON THEMATIC SHAPES

So far, in discussing aspects of serial usage, we have made no attempt to use melodic material in a consistent and economical manner. All thematic material has resulted from the moulding of serial note-groups into what have been considered the most suitable and expressive melodic phrases. But there has been no deliberate creation of thematic relationships between the parts, which have retained complete independence. Such so-called 'athematic' writing, though common enough with Webern and his followers, is naturally avoided by other composers who require greater thematic definition or the possibility of working with motif-relationships.

A completely different form of serial usage is that of developing each part from short 'motifs' which are usually formed from the most prominent note-group in the series, but sometimes comprise no more than its most characteristic interval.

For instance, the series of Seiber's *Ulysees* (Ex. 20) is particularly suited to a composition in which all motif-ideas are derived from various transformations of the three- and four-note groups which form the basis of the series. As we have already seen, the series is made up of an 'original' note-group comprising a rising minor third and semitone and its three variants 'RI', 'I', and 'R'.

In the following example, all thematic shapes are derived from the original three-note group and its variants. The minor third is frequently inverted to become a major sixth and similarly the semitone becomes a major seventh or minor ninth. Such inversions are naturally necessary in order not only to avoid thematic monotony, but to allow exploitation of the larger, more powerful intervals:

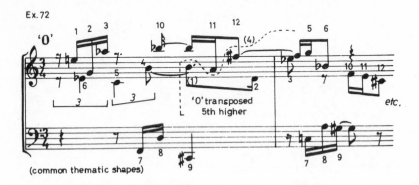

Ex. 72

Here the 'O' version is followed by its transposition to a perfect fifth above. It will be seen that overlapping of the two series has been achieved by using the B (middle part) in bar 1 as the fourth note of the original series and also the first of the transposed version. This has allowed melodic extension of the middle part into a five-note phrase. Similarly in the upper voice F♯ has been used as both the last note of the original series and the fourth of the transposed version. Such melodic extensions are naturally necessary to avoid the monotony of exclusively three-note phrases and at the same time the 'flow' of various serial forms is facilitated.

With such a series as that of Webern's Songs, Op. 23 (Ex. 27), however, there are no common thematic shapes running throughout the series. If it is desired to write music built on 'motifs' with such a series, it is best to select a characteristic note-group, such as the first four notes, as main thematic material, and try to make the rest of the series conform to the same general thematic pattern:

Ex. 73

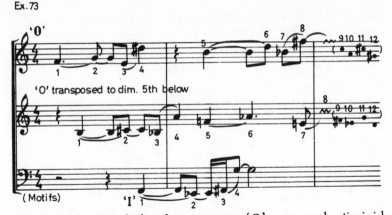

In this example, using 'O' in the upper part, 'O' transposed a diminished fifth below in the middle voice and 'I' at original pitch in the bass, it is obvious that thematic unity is easily retained in the first four notes of each part. But thereafter the motif-relationships tend to disintegrate because the same successions of intervals do not recur in the rest of the series. The only way to obtain the same four-note designs from the rest of the series is by considerable manipulation. To a great extent, therefore, the use of a series is a cumbersome method of writing music of common thematic shapes (unless the series is specifically designed for the purpose) and it would be more logical to abandon the serial method in favour of a free form of composition.

EXPANSION INTO NUMEROUS PARTS

We will now return to the method of expanding music into many and varying numbers of parts as in the example from Webern's *Zwei Lieder*, Op. 19 (Ex. 65). For this purpose we will again use the three rhythms which have formed the basis of Exx. 66–71. In the following illustration, the horizontal-vertical method of serial usage has been adopted, using 'O' followed by 'RI' of Webern's Songs, Op. 23:

(Expansion into numerous parts)

As will be seen, the number of parts fluctuates constantly. Single-note designs are used to form melodic outlines, contrasting with chords of varying density. In the brief space of a single bar, the music varies in density from a minimum of two contemporaneous notes to a maximum of seven. The second note of 'RI' (A) has had to be omitted as this note is already present in the lower stave.

There is no reason why the rhythmic patterns should not be inverted:

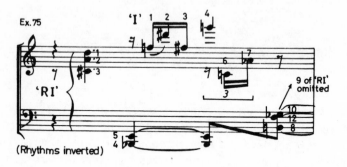

Here the 'I' version is used for a melodic outline in the upper part. The lower parts are formed from a horizontal-vertical use of 'RI'. The ninth note (G) of 'RI' is omitted as this is already present in the upper part.

In both Exx. 74 and 75, there is an event in the use of the horizontal-vertical method which has previously not occurred. That is, several notes are sounded simultaneously and we are met with the problem of how to order them. Some composers prefer to retain a strict order of the series in a vertical sense when two or more notes sound together. Sometimes notes are strictly ordered downwards (as notes 3 to 5 on the second beat of Ex. 74) or upwards (as 9 and 10 on the third beat). However, much better results are sure to be forthcoming if a free ordering is allowed in vertical note-combinations.

SCHOENBERG'S SERIES

Aware of the difficulty of avoiding octaves and false relations of the octave when using combinations of various forms of the series, Schoenberg attempted to eliminate this problem by constructing special series. These were usually built so that the original version had a special relationship with the inversion at a fifth below. The first six notes in the original were made to occur as notes 7 to 12 of the transposed inversion, *but in different order*. Similarly notes 7 to 12 in the original formed the first six notes of the transposed inversion, again ordered differently. This meant that the inversion transposed to a fifth below could be used as an accompaniment to the original series, with the maximum guarantee against producing octaves, as long as the two series moved more or less in parallel.

By changing the position of the fifth and tenth notes, the series used in our exercises (Ex. 27) can be made to conform with such requirements:

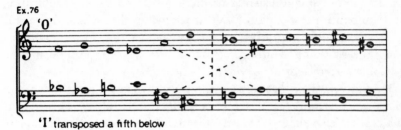

Ex.76

'O'

'I' transposed a fifth below

As will be seen, the same notes in each version are well separated, except for the fifth and eighth of each series. Using these two series together we find it quite easy to avoid octaves or any suggestion of false relations of the octave:

Ex.77

'O'

'I' transposed a fifth below

Unfortunately such series are only successful in their purpose if both original and transposed inverted versions move always in parallel. As soon as they cease to do so, they are as likely to produce octaves as any other series. It is obvious that in the end, such specially constructed series have proved to be of limited value and their principles have not been widely applied by other composers. However, the fact that Schoenberg devised such a series is proof that he recognized the existence of a defect in the serial method—that with combinations of various serial forms, strict ordering is not always possible—and tried to overcome it.

COMMENTS ON SERIAL MANIPULATION

As we have already seen in the few simple examples in this chapter, it has frequently been necessary to resort to serial manipulation in order to produce satisfactory results. This re-ordering of the series varies in extent. Sometimes it amounts to no more than the omission of a note in one part because it already exists in another. Occasionally it amounts to a complete re-organization of the serial note-order so as to eradicate an undesirable combination of sounds (such as triadic formations or note-combinations which produce poor tension-flow). It is obvious that where the normal succession of notes is disturbed (by serial manipulation), any notes omitted from the series must be introduced as soon afterwards as possible, in order to maintain consistent use of the total-chromatic.

But the very fact that serial manipulation is so frequently necessary points to a certain defect in the serial method. One of the cardinal principles on which serialism is based—that all elements of a composition are to be derived from a fixed succession of twelve different notes—proves in practice to be frequently impractical. It would be most unwise to maintain a strict, inflexible ordering of the series in our compositions, ignoring that possibility of improvement which serial manipulation allows. Manipulation of the series is in reality not only a means of perfecting a defective method, it is also one of the first steps which lead towards the complete relaxation of serial usage. For it introduces that element of free choice which in the end can lead to free twelve-note composition, in which the use of the series is abandoned in favour of a free use of the total-chromatic. However, full discussion of such topics is at present premature and must be delayed till our final chapter.

8. TWELVE-NOTE HARMONY

Twelve-note Harmony. Tonality and Atonality in Serial Music. Harmony and Tension Control. Harmonic Material and its Classification. The Ordering of Chordal Components and their Registers. Tone Colour, Dynamics, and Chordal Tension. Disposition of the Series in Harmonic Formations. Octaves and False Relations of the Octave in Twelve-note Harmony. Controlling the Harmonic Equilibrium with a Free Part.

TWELVE-NOTE HARMONY

Theory always lags well behind practice and this is especially the case where harmony is concerned. No theorist ever gave a complete picture of renaissance harmonic usage till later times. Bach never found any ready-made formulas for his magical chromatic progressions in any text book. In fact, a great deal of long-established harmonic practice has never been adequately codified until comparatively recently.

To attempt a full analysis and codification of twelve-note harmony at the present moment seems futile and doomed to failure. This is a task for the future. For the moment, the magnitude of the task seems immeasurable. There are over 4000 possible 'chords' available in the total-chromatic, that is, groups of notes varying from two to twelve in number. But this refers only to the *contents* of each chord, and ignores the many possible ways of ordering the contents. Here the problem magnifies, for the greater the number of notes in a chord, the greater the number of ways of arranging these notes. For instance, though the notes of a three-note chord can only be arranged in six patterns, a six-note group can be arranged in 720 patterns, and an eight-note chord in 40,320 patterns. In fact the total number of ways of ordering the contents of all chords of up to twelve notes is of course many millions. Furthermore, the problem increases still further when we consider the actual register of each note, for every sound can be placed in any one of at least seven octaves.

So far we have only considered the complexity of the problem with regard to the *vertical* grouping of notes. But harmony is the result of chord progressions—the *horizontal* relationship of one note-group with another. If we find difficulty in grasping the full potentialities of the myriad vertical arrangements of twelve notes, how can we possibly anticipate all the horizontal relationships between so many vertical combinations? At present, we seem faced with the impossible.

Our problem, for the moment, is more elementary. It is not so much that of understanding all the mass of harmonic material at our disposal, but of deciding whether to recognize that any harmonic problem exists at all. Schoenberg is said to have 'liquidated' tonality as long ago as 1908. Later he was to call his serial ideas a 'method of composing with twelve notes which are related only to one another'. This implies that combinations of notes are in no way related to one another through conventional harmonic procedures, and that these are to be excluded. Yet evidence of the continued presence of traditional tonal usage (according to the major and minor key systems) is abundantly present in his own work.

Today, many composers take the easy way out by refusing to recognize the existence of any harmonic problem. They disregard any relationship between the 'tempered' intervals of the twelve-note series and the old 'natural' intervals. Any consideration of the tonal implications of intervals is regarded as not only irrelevant, but quite undesirable. H. H. Stuckenschmidt writes 'When tonality is eliminated, intervals then become abstract building stones which may be added to one another without any relation to a common key centre'.[1] But is tonality only 'eliminated' from the composer's mind, or is it really eliminated in the music? We shall see the real truth of this in the next section.

However, at the present time, if we were to consider the harmonic implications of every note we write according to traditional tonal concepts, we would have a herculean task. But this does not mean that we are at liberty to heap notes together in complete disregard for the audible result.

We should combine sounds in such a way that whether they produce consonance or dissonance, stable or unstable harmonies, they should not only sound inevitable, they should make sense. Whether we do it by instinct or by orderly reasoning, we should make *harmony*—those successions of note groupings which *do not offend musical reason*, however complex the result.

This is the harmony we are concerned with here—not the limited field enclosed within the tonal confines of major and minor key systems, but the artistic use of all the myriad possibilities of the total-chromatic. *This is twelve-note harmony.* Later on we will establish a few essential principles which will serve as lode-stars in the navigation of this largely uncharted territory.

---

[1] *Musical Quarterly* (New York), January 1963.

The use of a twelve-note series does not automatically produce 'atonal' music. The reverse is often the case. In fact, some of Schoenberg's serial works seem to admit tonal centres to an extent which he hardly tolerated in his earlier period of free atonalism. One wonders if he was aware of this at first. Later, in his 'American Period' he certainly sought to align serialism with more traditional types of music and harmonic techniques. But in 1927, when his serial writing usually aimed at producing an atonal norm, one wonders whether the opening to the Adagio of his Third String Quartet deliberately aimed at producing tonal zones or whether they occurred by accident:

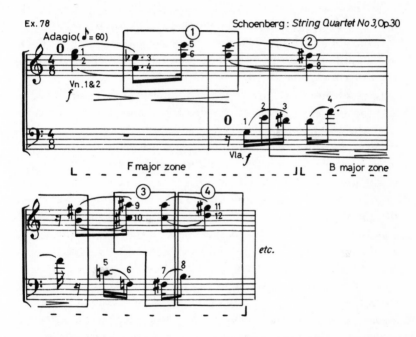

Ex. 78 Schoenberg : *String Quartet No 3, Op.30*

Apart from a few 'roving harmonies' (which fit easily into tonal schemes in any case) the music can be divided into two well defined tonal zones of F major and B major.[2] (It is worth noting that in twelve-note or serial

[2]As both the chord of F major and that of B major occur with their minor sevenths, it would be quite legitimate to regard them as dominants of B♭ major and E major respectively. However, as in this context neither chord reveals a strong tendency to move on to its 'tonic' resolution (in fact neither does so) it seems preferable to discount to some extent the weak influence of the sevenths and regard both chords as key centres. In fact the B major chord, rather than moving in the direction of a tonic E, moves on to its own dominant chord (F♯ major).

music, if tonalities occur, they are usually a tritone apart—for the obvious reason that the scale of one tonality contains all the chromatic elements missing from the scale of the other.) Particularly prominent in Ex. 78 are the chords of F major with its minor seventh (1), B major seventh (2), F♯ major (3) and a diminished triad (4) within the same tonal sphere. The tritone relationship between F major and B major (i.e. the most distant tonal relationship that is possible) is the only factor which makes this music any different from that using a system of traditional chromatic harmony. The tritone relationship between two keys always tends to have a certain 'obscuring' effect in key relationships, and is therefore mostly avoided in traditional harmony.

We have already noted (in Exx. 9 and 11) how Berg and Dallapiccola have deliberately introduced strong tonal elements into their serial writing. The intention is clearly that of bridging the gap between traditional and serial music, attenuating the atonal tendencies of the latter, and creating an equilibrium of tonal and non-tonal elements.

But with Anton Webern, the case is different. He is usually recognized as being the one member of the Viennese school who always set out to eliminate any possibility of traditional tonal associations in his work. As we have seen, his series are usually designed to eliminate any tonal groupings. A glance through his Variations Op. 27 for piano will reveal that practically all his chords contain notes in semitone relationship (usually as major sevenths and minor ninths) and if they are of more than two notes, there is almost always a tritone interval present. In short, his chords are deliberately obscure, designed to produce an atonal norm throughout. So are the horizontal successions of notes. Yet we do not need to look far to see the lurking spectre of tonality just below the obscuring layer of non-tonal associations. The opening 'thematic' section of the last movement of Webern's Symphony Op. 21 offers a striking example of serial music which has obviously been designed to give a completely atonal effect, but which, in reality, is only just one remove from being entirely in one key:

Ex.79   Webern: *Symphony*, Op. 21

Theme - Molto tranquillo (♩=54)   rhythmic mirror

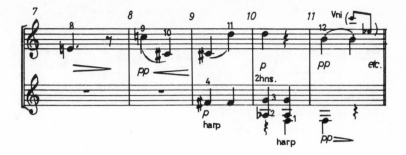

But before revealing this tonal background, it is worth dwelling on this example for a moment to appraise it purely from a serialist point of view, that is, from Webern's own viewpoint. The passage is a rhythmic mirror construction, with several ingenious points of technique which, however, do not concern us here. From a harmonic point of view, Webern has created movement away from the relatively stable tritone F–B in bar 1, through varying degrees of tension (and therefore relative harmonic instability) and back to the same neutral interval in bar 11. The tension degrees are carefully graded. From the neutral tritone (bar 1) the music moves through a zone of chromatic tension (bar 2) back to relaxation (G–C, in bar 3). Beginning again on G in bar 4 (and therefore with minimum tension) the music then moves through a melodic pattern which suggests chromatic harmonies (G, F♯, B♭ and E) and therefore an attenuated degree of tension, to the central pivot of the whole passage—the tritone interval A–E♭, where the same degree of neutral tension is achieved as in bar 1. However this is rightly passed over quickly (so that the harmonic flow does not sag), and the music then procedes through the same tension degrees *in reverse* back to the same neutral F–B as the beginning. From the serialist's tension-relaxation concept (the only means of evaluating chordal progressions if tonal concepts are ignored), the passage is therefore an ideal ebb and flow of tension and repose, both being held in a delicate equilibrium.

But in reality there is a tonal background to this passage, which with the violin entry in bar 11 leaps out into clear definition—for bar 11 is a truncated full cadence in C minor. Naturally things are not quite as simple as all that. But if we omit the one note (F♯) which is the most complete denial of C (major or minor), the whole eleven bars can be written out to reveal the underlying presence of C tonality:

Of course, the notes are here disposed differently, but (except for the omission of F♯) the suggested harmonies are none other than those implied by Webern.

We have already noted in Schoenberg's Third String Quartet (Ex. 78) that the tritone relationship between the two tonalities (F and B) was the only factor which tended to obscure the clarity of key relationships. Again here, it is the tritone relationship of F♯ with the underlying C tonality which turns Webern's music away from a definite sense of key. The occurrence of F♯ in bars 4 and 9 is the major factor which disrupts the C tonality and preserves the atonal equilibrium.

This disrupting effect of the tritone is universal in twelve-note and serial music, and at this point it would be well to formulate a definite conclusion:

Any tendency for a tonality to emerge may be avoided by introducing a note three whole tones distant from the key note of that tonality.

This has led us rather far from the subject under discussion—tonality and atonality in twelve-note and serial music. But by now it will be abundantly clear that the use of a series does not preclude the existence of key centres, even when the composer's intention is to avoid any tonal suggestions.

Furthermore, it is certain that *given adequate control*, the series can be made to produce music which borders on the field of chromatic harmony, music which maintains a delicate tonal-atonal equilibrium, or music which is the complete negation of tonality, verging on 'atonal chaos'. Given adequate control, the composer should be able to move from one of these zones to another at will, thereby having wide expressive resources at his disposal. However, as will be seen later, it is this control which is so often lacking. The composer is dominated by the 'method'—in which case the music moves hapazardly between zones of tonality and non-tonality in ungainly fashion, and with crude and unpleasant results. We will refer to this again in the next section.

However, when serialism is abandoned, and free twelve-note writing is assumed, control of the harmonic field is much more certain. As long as there is a constant flow of all components of twelve-note space, and as long as note-successions avoid any possibility of tonal groupings, a perpetual pantonal equilibrium is guaranteed. Nothing happens by accident, only by intent. The 'chance' element of serialism is abandoned for the certitude of complete control. However, it is too early to discuss this in full, and the subject must be postponed until our final chapter.

HARMONY AND TENSION CONTROL

In the chapter on 'Writing in Two Parts' we have examined the various degrees of consonance, dissonance, and tension in intervals, and also the method of controlling tension in two-part writing. We have seen that by manipulation of the series, successions of intervals can be formed which give a satisfactory flow of tension, either towards a climax or to a point of stability and repose.

Precisely the same is true of music in any number of parts. And as long as there are zones of tension and repose smoothly interconnected, where the composer wants them, and of the right degree of intensity, we may be sure that not only have the dictates of tension control been satisfied, but that a good harmonic flow has been also provided. *For good harmonic flow is virtually the same thing as good tension flow.*

If we can dissociate harmony for a moment from its traditional alliance with major and minor keys, we then have the concept of harmony in twelve-note or serial music as being the tension relationship between one group of notes and another, and between various groups of notes in a whole passage. If the tension is mild (and the chords comparatively stable) the harmonic path is smooth. If the tension is acute (and the chords unstable) the harmony is harsh, though not necessarily displeasing. Bad aesthetic effect only occurs if the movement between zones of mild and acute tension is abrupt and ill-placed.

In the end, we can conclude that harmony is good tension-flow, and good tension-flow is harmony. They are almost identical from a practical compositional point of view when dealing with highly chromatic music of the type to which serialism belongs.

But, it may be objected, in the previous section care was taken to show that, in serial music, tonal centres can be either obviously present or very near the surface. Now it has just been stated that tonalities can be ignored, focusing attention on 'harmonic tension' rather than on harmony in any tonal sense.

The reason is purely one of convenience. All twelve-note harmonies, even the most complex atonal passages, have tonal foundations. Any chord, taken in isolation, has its 'resolution'. But at the moment, our knowledge of twelve-note harmony is so slight that we cannot give adequate tonal explanations of complex phenomena. If we were to seek tonal justifications for every note-grouping we write in serial or twelve-note music, composition would be a very slow and wearisome affair. The ponderousness of the 'method' would repress our creative faculties.

It is therefore much more practical to ignore key relationships and similar tonal considerations. By keeping control only of the tension-flow, composition can be greatly facilitated, and results are rapid and satisfactory. However, *audible* control is also essential for a perfect result. We cannot expect to hear everything we write, especially at first, and it is essential that students subject everything to audible control. This will reveal many unsuspected flaws, and by investigating the reason for every imperfection, we can adopt a useful process of self-tuition which has immense practical value, and in the long run is much more instructive than the works of any theorist.

Naturally, while keeping a vigilant eye on tension control, we must be careful that the atonal equilibrium is maintained, and that an unwanted perfect triad does not slip in by accident (we will see in a moment how this happens to Stravinsky). It is necessary also to watch for chords which are less obvious, yet still unambiguously related to key centres, such as diminished seventh chords, incomplete dominant sevenths, etc.

Of course, if we wish to write serial music which, like that of Berg, belongs to both the tonal and atonal worlds, the concept of harmony only through tension control is inadequate. Inevitably, where tonalities are concerned, tonal harmonic concepts will be used. They will probably have to be reconciled with many serial factors, in which case the compositional discipline will be unusually complex, much more so than is usually recognized, for the criteria of two opposing systems have constantly to be dovetailed into a new unity.

Before concluding this section it is necessary to give an example of faulty tension control, and the jarring results it can produce. Stravinsky in his *Canticum Sacrum* begins the third section 'Caritas' with an introduction for organ, woodwind, and brass. In the first six bars, a twelve-note series is given out alone in double octaves. The chromatic movement forms an evenly mild tension-flow. From the sixth to the tenth bar the music spreads out to four parts in smoothly flowing harmony of almost traditional character. But in the second half of bar 10 there is a sudden plunge into harsh discords:

These generate an unpleasantly acute tension, which is aggravated by the hard texture of double-reed woodwind and brass. The passage is full of semitonal dissonances. In the five-part chords which end each bar, all notes present are a semitone (or its inversion) distant from another note. The result seems somewhat brutal, especially in a passage which sets out to prepare us for a discourse on 'charity'. Such a passage would be justified if it illustrated some dramatic situation, as could easily occur in opera. But we are dealing here with music of a contemplative, non-dramatic character.

Five bars of fairly strong tension follow, and then comes another plunge, this time into complete consonance:

Ex. 82

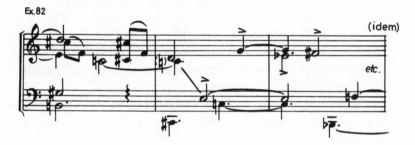

One can only form the opinion that the C major chord in such a situation is possibly fortuitous. In the midst of such a zone of strong dissonances, it causes a collapse in the tension flow which, fortunately is of only brief duration. As other serial parts of the *Canticum* contain similar passages of distorted tension-flow by the juxtaposition of excessive consonance and dissonance, it would seem that Stravinsky did not always observe problems of tension control in this work, and like so many other composers allowed the series to be completely responsible for musical results. Schoenberg's supposition that the twelve notes are related 'only to one another' can be taken too literally. As we have seen, they are related to a host of other factors as well.

Earlier in this chapter it was pointed out that the number of possible note groupings or 'chords' in the twelve-note system was over 4000. This referred only to the content of each chord, whereas the number of possible arrangements of the contents is virtually infinite.

Though it is neither practical nor useful to catalogue all possible chords, there is some purpose in examining the most simple groups of two, three, or four notes, and establishing their various tension degrees. The same principles can then be applied for chords of five notes or more. However, we must observe without delay that the tension degrees of even the most simple chords can undergo considerable modification, in certain circumstances which will be considered in due course.

Indeed the modification can be so radical that (in order to avoid misunderstanding) we must state categorically that the degrees of tension given in the following lists of chords are valid only for the chord formations as given, and not for any other ordering of the chordal components. The degrees of tension here given represent the *maximum* characteristics of the chords as given below, with the notes in close ordering. Any inversion of the chords, and the octave displacement of any note or notes, can radically change these maximum characteristics. This will be more fully discussed later. However, despite these reservations, the inclusion of the following lists of chords is indispensable, as the investigation of harmonic phenomena must begin with an examination of the maximum characteristics of simple note-groups. Once these maximum characteristics are known, discussion of any alteration of these characteristics can then follow as a logical and inevitable consequence.

In this section, degrees of tension have been classified in seven grades, according to the proportion of consonance and dissonance present.[3] They are indicated as follows:

cc = strong consonance
c = mild consonance
n = neutral
m = mild dissonance
s = strong dissonance
h = harsh dissonance
vh = very harsh dissonance

[3]It may be regarded as inconsistent to use the terms 'consonance' and 'dissonance' when key relationships and similar tonal considerations are ignored. Yet they are such characteristic qualities of intervals and chords either in tonal or atonal spheres and so accurately descriptive that we must still retain their use. Also, we so constantly find dissonance used as a term descriptive of harmonic tension, and consonance of harmonic repose, that we can hardly do otherwise than regard them as generally synonymous terms in twelve-note harmony.

Naturally, in these seven grades, the tension of 'cc' is regarded as zero, and 'vh' as maximum. In the following examples of two, three and four-note chords, many of the tension degrees given are somewhat arbitrary, depending on personal taste and the musical context. For instance, an isolated chord of the 'added sixth' (e.g. C, E, G, A) is mildly dissonant, but in a context of strong tension can appear completely consonant.

TWO-NOTE CHORDS

Ex.83

N.B.—(1) The minimum number of two-note chords based on C is six (i.e. the white notes shown above). However, inversions of these intervals are given (black notes) for the sake of completeness.
(2) These two-note chords can be transposed to any position in the chromatic scale. Thus the total number of possible two-note chords is 66.

THREE-NOTE CHORDS

Ex. 84

(chord marked 'x' has a limited number of transpositions)

N.B.—(1) This is the minimum number of three-note chords based on C. Transposed inversions of any chord are omitted—e.g. the minor triad CEA is omitted because this formation is already given in the form CE♭G.
(2) These three-note chords can be transposed to any position in the chromatic scale. The total number of possible three-note chords is 220.

FOUR-NOTE CHORDS

Ex. 85

(Chords marked 'x' have limited number of transpositions)

N.B.—(1) This is the minimum number of four-note chords based on C. Transposed versions of any chord are omitted—e.g. the chord CDFB is omitted because this formation is already given in the form CDβEβGβ.
(2) These four-note chords can be transposed to any position in the chromatic scale. The total number of possible four-note chords is 495.

1. It will be seen that while in two-note chords the tensions are fairly well mixed, with a bias towards consonance, and in three-note chords there is a slight preponderance of strong dissonances, by far the greater number of four-note chords have considerable degrees of dissonance. The proportion of dissonant note groups increases in chords of five and more notes. Multi-note chords therefore tend to be uniformly dissonant. The more notes there are in the chords, the less possibility is there of tension contrast. But by this very lack of tension contrast, uniformity of tension flow is more easily obtained.

2. All chords which form whole-tone groups have 'neutral' tension. While in two-part writing we have observed the variable nature of the tritone, in atonal music of three or more parts whole-tone groups have a tension degree midway between mild consonance and mild dissonance. Though in the close formations given in these examples, whole-tone groups are dissonant, in practice the notes are often spread out and thereby lose a great deal of tension.

3. As almost all note-groups are given in their closest formation, their degrees of tension are at maximum level. As we have noted in the section on 'The Importance of Register' (Chapter 6) 'the varying degrees of tension between notes comprising the various intervals become more uniform in proportion to the distance separating the notes'. Similarly, in chordal constructions, the varying degrees of consonance and dissonance are less perceptible when notes are far apart. This is strikingly illustrated by comparing the harsh dissonance of C, D♭, and E in close formation as at 'a' below, with the almost consonant effect of the same notes spread out at 'b':

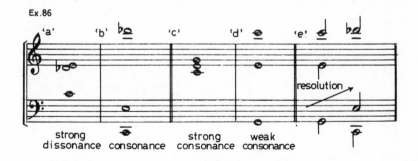

Ex.86

Furthermore, the close formation of a major triad in root position ('c'), the strongest consonance of all, loses a considerable part of its consonance and harmonic stability when spread out as at 'd'.

73

Now if 'd' is followed by 'b' as at 'e', there is a sense of 'resolution', as the progression is from a weak, unstable consonance to a stronger one. This is due not only to the wide spread of the notes, but to their vertical ordering, which dictates the stability of 'b' and the instability of 'd'.

Here therefore we have a remarkable phenomenon: by inversion *a strong dissonance has become more consonant than the strongest consonance.* This indicates that the tension degrees set out in the tables of two-, three-, and four-note chords can in certain circumstances be subject to considerable modification. These tension degrees are only valid when note groups are in close formation. The characteristics of intervals (their consonance, dissonance, stability, or instability) are annulled by wide differences of register. Furthermore, the characteristics of chords depends considerably on the vertical ordering of the component notes. These factors are obviously so important that we must now subject them to further scrutiny.

THE ORDERING OF CHORDAL COMPONENTS AND THEIR REGISTERS

1. Three-note chords

Returning to the three-note chord used in the previous example (CD♭E), these notes can be disposed vertically in six different orders:

$$\begin{array}{ccc}
C & D\flat & E \\
C & E & D\flat \\
D\flat & C & E \\
D\flat & E & C \\
E & C & D\flat \\
E & D\flat & C
\end{array}$$

As each of these notes can be placed in seven different octaves or more, there are obviously hundreds of different ways these chords can be written. To investigate all these possibilities would be confusing and superfluous. To bring out the main facts it is sufficient to write them in the following six dispositions:

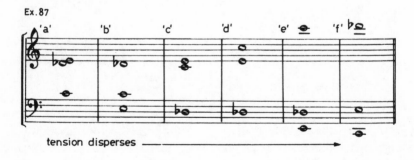

Ex.87

tension disperses ⟶

Here the chords have been so disposed in order and in register as to form a gradual change from strong dissonance and tension ('a') to comparatively strong consonance and repose ('f'). The gradual dispersal of dissonance and accumulation of consonance have been obtained through the following sequence of alterations in the disposition of the notes:

Chord 'b'—The 'strongest' interval (C–E) has been put in the 'strongest' position—the bass, though it is inverted in the form of a less consonant sixth. The dissonance C–D♭ is not changed.

Chord 'c'—The semitonal dissonance C–D♭ is attenuated by increasing the interval to a major seventh. The 'strongest' interval is now in the upper parts.

Chord 'd'—The dissonance C–D♭ is further attenuated by raising C an octave. The 'strongest' interval is still in the upper parts.

Chord 'e'—The dissonance C–D♭ is further attenuated by raising C to almost three octaves distance. Consonance is increased by forming a strong sixth (E–D♭) in the bass.

Chord 'f'—The dissonance C–D♭ is further attenuated by placing these notes more than four octaves apart. Consonance is increased by placing the 'strongest' interval (C–E) in the bass, and as a strongly consonant interval (the tenth). C is also the natural harmonic bass of the note group.

From this experiment three factors are strongly evident:

1. *Tension decreases in proportion to the size of the interval separating the dissonant notes.*

2. *Consonance is increased by placing the 'strongest' interval in the bass, even though it may be in an inverted position.*

3. *Consonance is further increased by placing the natural harmonic bass of the 'strongest' interval as the lowest note of the chord.*

2. Four-note chords

We will now see how these principles apply when used with dissonant four-note chords. Unfortunately, as the components of four-note chords can be disposed in 24 different orders (and each note in any octave register) we cannot pretend to conduct a complete investigation. But a few typical examples will suffice to draw conclusions. For this experiment we will use the 'very dissonant' group CD♭E♭E♮. For notational simplicity D♭ is sometimes written as C♯ and E♭ as D♯:

Ex.88

tension disperses ——————————————————————————————→

The above nine chords have been arranged in gradually decreasing degrees of dissonance from left to right. Each note in the chord has been used twice as a bass. The principles discovered in dealing with three-note chords are all confirmed. It would be tedious to analyse every chord, but one main detail should be pinpointed: the overwhelming supremacy of 'h' and 'i' as consonant chords spotlights C as a bass of special significance. It would be hard to understand why 'h' should be more consonant than 'g' (the notes are arranged in more 'dissonant' order in 'h', and there is no 'strong' interval in the bass) were it not for the fact that C, as the harmonic bass note of the strongest interval (C–E) of the note-group, is the bass note most certain to create consonant harmony.

In every chord we use there is a strongest interval and in this a strongest 'key' note. If this note is placed as the bass of a chord, consonance is most assured. However, if strong tension is required the influence of the 'strongest bass' and 'strongest interval' must be liquidated by dispersion.

Before we leave the four-note group CD♭D♯E there is still one observation to make. These sounds can be grouped into two consonant intervals, C♮E♭ and C♯E♮, which are, however, dissonant with each other. To disperse the harsh tension of these notes in close formation, it is not sufficient merely to dispose the notes as two consonant intervals as in 'a' or 'b':

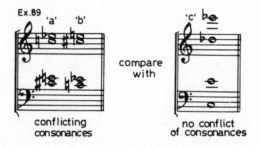

Ex.89

compare with

conflicting consonances

no conflict of consonances

Both 'a' and 'b' are almost as tense as the chord in close formation. Neither concord is able to establish predominance, and the result is a harshly dissonant "conflict of consonances". Compare these with 'c' which is comparatively relaxed and euphonious, because only one consonant interval (E C) is given prominence and is put in the bass, while the other dissonant elements are dispersed above at a sufficient distance.

However, the 'conflict of consonances' can be mitigated by placing the two consonant intervals more than an octave apart:

Ex.90

conflict of
consonances
attenuated

We can therefore deduce that:

If a note group can be formed into two or more consonant intervals which are dissonant with each other, tension will be created if these consonant intervals are placed close together. It will be dispersed if they are separated, or one interval is allowed to predominate.

3. Multi-note chords

All the principles noted with regard to three- and four-note chords apply also to chords of five or more notes. However, one more factor in multiple-note chords must be illustrated, and to do this we will write various groupings of an eight-note chord which embraces all the semitones from C to G:

Ex.91

tension disperses ⎯⎯⎯⎯⎯⎯⎯⎯⎯⎯⎯➤

Naturally, in close formation ('a') this chord is tightly packed with tension. This is gradually dispersed through 'b', 'c', 'd', and 'e' by separating dissonances more and more, and placing consonant intervals in the bass.

However, I would like to focus attention most on the three most consonant formations 'f', 'g', and 'h'. When considering which note will make the 'strongest bass' (and consequently form the most consonant chord) we have three possibilities:

(1) the lowest note of a fifth: (C, F, F♯, and G are the only possible notes)
(2) the lowest note of a major third: (C, D♭, D, and E♭ are the only possible notes)
(3) the lowest note of a complete triad: (C is the only possible note)

In case (1) F would seem the 'strongest note' as in the traditional tonal cycle of fifths it is more towards the 'flatter', sub-dominant side than the other notes. In case (2) D♭ seems the 'strongest note', for the same reason. In case (3) C is the only possible note, as only one major triad can be formed.

As a fifth is a more stable consonance than a third, one would expect a bass of type (1) to form a more stable, consonant chord than a bass of type (2). However, of the two chords 'f' and 'g', the one having the fifth at the bottom ('f') seems the least consonant. This is because the lowest notes F, C, and G in 'f' are tonally vague and form a less defined harmonic foundation than the powerful tenth D♭–F in 'g'.

But the chord with a bass of type (3) proves to be the most stable and consonant of all. This is because it has been possible to form the complete chord of C major as a powerful foundation for the whole note-complex. As all other dissonances are well dispersed in upper registers, it will certainly be felt that chord 'h' is almost smoothly pleasant by comparison with the jarring clash of all the semitones together in 'a'.

From this investigation we can conclude that: *the tension of multi-note groups can be attenuated most if a major chord (preferably in root position) forms its foundation.*

WARNING

All the stress in this section has been on the creation of consonance, harmonic stability, and euphony. Our attention has been given to the liquidation of tension and not to its creation. This may have created the false impression that all note-groupings must be ordered in their most consonant formations. This is by no means so. In atonal music tense, dissonant formations are needed just as much as relaxed, consonant ones.

The reason for stressing the formation of the more consonant grouping of chords is merely the simple fact that in serial and twelve-note music it is easy enough to make a discordant jangle of notes, but to mould the material into a 'concord of sweet sounds' needs considerable artistry and technical skill. The perpetual recurrence of the total-chromatic tends of its own accord towards atonal chaos. We must learn to control this tendency and by our knowledge of the ordering of chordal components graduate the tension-flow to the exact degree of harmonic stability or instability, dissonance or consonance, required at any given point in our compositions.

It may seem something of a paradox that those triadic formations which elsewhere have been carefully avoided should now have been reintroduced to some degree. The truth is that triadic formations can be quite eliminated in forming harmony of a tense, dissonant nature, but at points where greater euphony and relaxation are needed we cannot ignore the fact that the more consonant (and therefore frequently triadic) harmonic elements must be allowed to emerge, while factors which produce greater stress must be subdued. However this in no way implies that we need resort to the traditional artifices of key schemes, modulations, transitions, etc. We are merely using the consonance of triadic formations in order to take advantage of its very valuable power of liquidating tension.

4. Chords of twelve and more notes

Chords which contain all twelve notes of the total-chromatic need not be completely dissonant. In fact, if dissonances are widely dispersed and a strongly 'tonal' note-grouping is placed in the lower region, the result is excellent and not unpleasant. The same is true of chords containing more than twelve notes.

However, in these multi-note chords, tension easily tends towards uniformity. The only means of creating varying degrees of tension is to contrast the more concordant note-groupings with tense chords which contain more or less dense semitonal clusters in various registers.

Naturally, in chords containing more than twelve notes, unless micro-intervals are used (quarter-tones, etc.), some notes have to be duplicated. In this case it is best to place duplicated notes in widely different registers, so that prominent octave effects are eliminated.

Inevitably, multi-note chords are usually spread over several octaves. The more notes these chords contain, the nearer the general sound effect approaches to that of the 'white sound' in electronic music.

TONE COLOUR, DYNAMICS, AND CHORDAL TENSION

Tone colour has a great influence on the eventual tension quality of chords. If dissonant intervals are played by instruments with strong upper partials (and therefore of strident tone quality) their dissonant quality will be exaggerated and therefore their tension increased. If they are played by mellow-sounding instruments, their tension will be diminished. Strong dynamics also exaggerate tension in intervals.

By these two factors, one can easily imagine that a chord of only mild dissonance (e.g. CDF) can be considerably more tense if played loudly by three trumpets, than a very harsh dissonance (e.g. CD♭D♯E) played softly by muted violins.

These factors are most useful in dealing with multi-note chords, for we can either 'colour' the dissonances strongly or subdue them, bring out consonant factors or hide them away behind the elements of greater stress.

DISPOSITION OF THE SERIES IN HARMONIC FORMATIONS

The twelve-note series can be used both *horizontally*, as melody, or *vertically*, to create harmonic formations. In melody, the order of the twelve notes of the series is usually carefully observed. But employed vertically to create harmony, the series is used with much greater freedom. There are three main reasons for this:

1. As melody, the series can be aurally identified. It retains its own individuality. But used vertically as harmony, we cannot follow the simultaneous presentation of various serial groupings. The series therefore loses its identity, and to retain the order of its notes in harmonic formations has no audible or practical value.

2. Any particular group of notes may be so ordered as to produce many varied effects of harmony and tension. It is therefore important to retain freedom in the vertical ordering of any note formation in order to create harmonic variety and a satisfactory tension flow in the general harmonic context.

3. Freedom in vertical ordering is often necessary for practical reasons, e.g. the range of voices or instruments, the span of the hand on the keyboard or fingerboard, etc.

Various ways of ordering the series in harmonic formations will now be illustrated, writing in four parts for voices. The series used (from Webern's *Das Augenlicht*, Op. 26) will be as follows:

Ex.92

from Webern's *Das Augenlicht*, Op.26

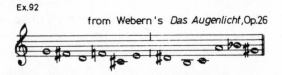

HARMONY FORMED FROM THE SERIES IN STRICT VERTICAL ORDERINGS

Here the notes of the series are used in strict order downwards (as in 'a') or upwards (as in 'b'):

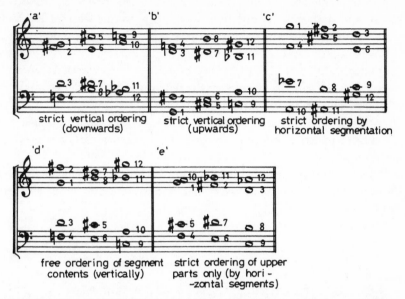

strict vertical ordering
(downwards)

strict vertical ordering
(upwards)

strict ordering by
horizontal segmentation

free ordering of segment
contents (vertically)

strict ordering of upper
parts only (by hori-
-zontal segments)

HARMONY FORMED FROM HORIZONTAL STREAMS OF SERIAL SEGMENTS

Here the soprano part is formed from notes 1, 2, and 3, the alto from
4, 5, and 6 and so on (as in 'c').

HARMONY FORMED FROM SERIAL SEGMENTS WITH CONTENTS FREELY
ORDERED

Each chord consists of the same elements as in 'a' and 'b', but freely
ordered (as in 'd'). This is naturally the same procedure as a free vertical
ordering of segments of the series.

HARMONY FORMED FROM A PARTIALLY FREE ORDERING OF THE SERIES

Strict order is only observed in the upper parts (soprano = 10, 11, 12
and alto 1, 2, 3), the lower parts have a free arrangement of the remaining
six notes (as in 'e').

HARMONY FORMED FROM A COMPLETELY FREE ORDERING OF THE SERIES

No strict order is observed. In reality this procedure is identical with
free twelve-note writing.

It will be seen that the strict vertical ordering in 'a' and 'b' has produced
ungrateful harmony, with acute degrees of tension, though 'b' is more
euphonious than 'a'. The horizontal streams of serial segments 'c' should
have fallen into very much the same atonal pattern as 'a' and 'b'. But per-
verse 'chance' has thrown out three chords of almost completely tonal
implications. (The first chord is that of F ninth, the second that of F♯
major, the third is a whole-tone group. The only note out of place is the
B in the second chord.)

The unpredictable results of strict ordering are therefore amply illustrated, and though strict ordering may appeal to our sense of logic, this must not blind us to the unsatisfactory nature of the harmonic results.

On the other hand, the free ordering of the contents of serial segments ('d') has produced more satisfactory harmony. Excessive dissonances are well separated and the parallel sixths between tenor and bass make for harmonic coherence and direction.

In the partially free ordering of the series ('e'), though the upper parts are subject to strict ordering, freedom in the lower parts has produced good harmony.

When harmony is formed from a completely free ordering of the series (or of the total-chromatic in free twelve-note writing), naturally any result can be obtained at will.

Here are three examples:

Ex.94

It will be seen that while 'f' is no more than conventional chromatic harmony, 'g' is adjusted to an atonal equilibrium and 'h' is designed to produce a considerable degree of tension.

HARMONY FORMED FROM HORIZONTAL STREAMS OF VARIOUS FORMS OF A SERIES

Harmony may be formed in this way by homophonic writing, or by counterpoint.

In HOMOPHONIC WRITING, each voice may consist of transposed forms of the same version of the series, producing parallel voice parts:

Ex.95   Webern: *Das Augenlicht,* Op. 26

Though this produces a pleasantly euphonious result, all the chords being first inversions of minor chords with added ninths, this is not twelve-note harmony. In this group of twenty notes, it will be found that while F and F♯ are each used three times, C, D♯, G, and A are used only once and G♯ not at all. Furthermore, false relations of the octave (as indicated by the dotted lines) are abundant. We can only interpret such a passage as being in conventional chromatic harmony.

Here Webern uses a very simple form of homophonic writing, but it is more usual for the voices of the horizontal 'streams' to consist of more than one version of the series. The fact that transpositions of only one version of the series produces parallelisms is a limiting factor, for parallelisms can only be used over short periods without falling into banality.

It is more usual in homophonic writing for horizontal voices to be made up of more than one form of the series. However, this can cause difficulties which it will be best to illustrate by re-writing the above passage, beginning on the same notes, but using the 'O', 'I', 'R', and 'R.I.' versions in each voice:

Ex.96

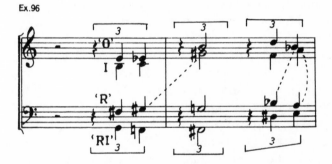

In this group of twenty notes, the total-chromatic is much more evenly spread than in Webern's example, though C♯ is not used.

But there are not only two false relations of the octave, there is also a real octave (A) in the last chord.

The worst feature, however, is the bad harmonic flow, for the third and fifth chords are now completely opposed to the mild tension degrees of the other chords.

These are the difficulties of homophonic writing using various forms of the series—bad harmonic flow, fortuitous octaves and false relations of the octave.

MULTIPLE PARALLELISMS

However, before leaving this section, it must be noted that multiple parallelisms moving in contrary motion can often produce harmonic coherence and forward harmonic flow which eliminate any bad effects of fortuitous octaves and false relations which may occur. In the following example there are three upper parts in fourths and two inner parts in minor thirds which move in parallel motion, while the three lower parts (forming an 'extended' augmented triad) move in contrary motion to the upper parts:

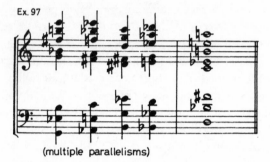

Ex. 97

(multiple parallelisms)

This kind of multiple parallelism, using different transpositions of the series, is sometimes used by those composers who wish to preserve a more conventional harmonic feeling in their work.

Harmony resulting from STRICT COUNTERPOINT where the voices use various forms of the series is subject to the same defects as in homophonic writing which uses various serial forms. As, in strict counterpoint, the imitations should be exact and the note durations are fixed by the leading voice, it is very difficult to regulate the harmonic flow and to avoid octaves and false relations of the octave.

In the following choral example from Stravinsky's *Canticum Sacrum* the music consists of a four-part canon. The leading voice (tenor) is imitated by the trumpet in augmentation, the alto entry is an inversion of the tenor part, while the discant imitates the tenor but inverts most of the intervals:

Apart from the octave between tenor and discant at the beginning of the fifth bar, and the false relations of the octave in bars four and five, the harmonic flow is badly regulated. The first four bars contain almost diatonic note-associations, except for the two semitone clashes at 'a' and 'b'. But the fifth bar plunges into harsh semitone relationships which create harmony of an altogether different character. We are given the impression that it is not the composer who has controlled the harmony, but that it is just a chance-born child of contrapuntal circumstances.

As harmony is the *real* audible result of the combination of various contrapuntal voices, it is more important than contrapuntal exactitude. Bad harmonic flow and octaves (both real and by false relations) must be avoided, and the only way to do this is to refuse to allow the series complete domination. As any combination of series produces octaves or bad harmony sooner or later, the only procedure we can follow is to omit any note which causes a defect in part-writing or harmony. If serial correctness is aimed at, this omitted note can then be included in the same voice as soon afterwards as is convenient.

In *free* counterpoint, however, these problems are easier to avoid. By free counterpoint we intend various independent voice parts, not in imitation, which have not to follow a strict pattern laid down by a leading voice. In free counterpoint it is therefore easy to adjust the note durations in each part, so that octaves can be avoided and a good flow of harmonic tension provided.

HARMONY FORMED FROM MELODY AND ACCOMPANIMENT

Not infrequently serial music is formed from a principal melody which uses one form of a series, and an accompaniment using another form of the same series:

Ex.99   Webern : *Three Songs*, Op.23

In this example, while the voice part sings a melody comprising the 'O' version of the series beginning on F, the piano accompaniment uses various other forms—the 'R', 'RI', and 'O' forms of the same series beginning on B.

It is worth noticing that Webern's writing here contains none of the defects we have just observed in Stravinsky's *Canticum Sacrum*. The harmony maintains the same atonal equilibrium throughout. The tension-flow is even and not disrupted by any excessive contrasts of consonance and dissonance. There are no octaves or false relations of the octave. Where notes in the voice part are the same as in the accompaniment (G and E in bar 2, G♭ in bar 4) Webern is careful to sound them at the unison and not at the octave. In bar 3 where the piano should begin the 'O' version on B, this note is omitted as the voice has B as an essential melodic note on the last beat of the bar. In any case, Webern takes care to remove the B from the piano part (l.h.) as this note has just been played in the right hand as I of 'RI'. It was therefore all the more necessary to avoid repetition of this note.

In writing melody and accompaniment, it will usually be found necessary to follow Webern's procedure—to keep the serial form of the melody intact, and to make any necessary omissions or modifications in the accompanying parts.

OCTAVES AND FALSE RELATIONS OF THE OCTAVE IN TWELVE-NOTE HARMONY

As already pointed out in the chapter on two-part writing, octaves should be avoided. The original objection to octaves was that they bring one note into prominence and thus tend to form a tonal centre. But if this is true, it was hardly logical to allow doubling of a note at the unison, for this can equally bring one note into prominence. In any case, we have seen that the creation of tonal centres, whether by calculation or by chance, is by no means uncommon in serial music.

The real root of the objection to octaves in serial music is to be found elsewhere. In any music of a highly chromatic nature (serial or otherwise) successful harmonic flow depends on good tension flow, and good tension flow requires that all the intervals within any chord should form within themselves a satisfactory equilibrium of tension. The presence of an octave destroys this tension equilibrium, as it predominates so strongly that other interval tensions are partly liquidated or eclipsed. The result is that any chord containing a prominent octave has a weak, insipid effect among other chords of atonal tension, and therefore causes a defective void in the harmonic flow. However, the disruptive effect of octaves is greatly reduced if the two notes which comprise the interval are widely separated, and in this way, especially in multi-note chords, any objection to them may to some extent be waived. The old objections to false relations of the octave (as tending to create tonal centres) can be equally over-ruled. The real objection to them is quite different. In highly chromatic music, the full power of every note-relationship can only be achieved if each note has the 'gloss of novelty'. Every note, as it occurs, whether in melody, or as a component part of harmony, must seem fresh and new. If one note is repeated too often, whether at the unison or in some other register, it becomes fatigued, its newness is dissipated. Here is the real objection to false relations of the octave—'note fatigue'. The mere fact that the same note appears in two adjacent chords is sufficient to diminish the full effect of the second chord.

This factor of 'note fatigue' needs vigilant attention. The sure way to avoid it is to keep the total-chromatic in constant circulation, to make sure that the same note does not recur too frequently in the same part (especially in the melody) or in adjacent chords, and to maintain variety in the register in which notes recur.

One last point with regard to note fatigue—if it is desired that any special chord or melody note should appear particularly strongly in some strategic position, the best strategy to adopt is to allow the note or notes in question to acquire 'freshness' by omitting them for some time previously. This is particularly necessary where a melody note or a chord must produce a sense of climax or of finality.

CONTROLLING THE HARMONIC EQUILIBRIUM WITH A FREE PART

Though the use of free parts does not fall into line with strict serial practice, it is possible to compose two or more important (serial) parts first, and then add a free part above or below (preferably the latter) which unifies the whole into a perfectly regulated harmonic equilibrium. This could be done using the serial method also in the note-order of the 'free' part, but the use of a strict note-order would create many difficulties. Some freedom of choice in note-order is essential if the functions of the free part are to be carried out with facility. As this procedure belongs more to the realm of free twelve-note composition, full discussion of this matter has been delayed until the final chapter, where it will be fully illustrated.

9. POLYPHONIC WRITING

Conventional Contrapuntal Forms. Rhythmic Counterpoints and Canons.
Free Counterpoints. Mirror Forms and Structures. Intelligibility.

Polyphonic writing has always been favoured by serial composers. Indeed contrapuntal styles are well suited to any highly chromatic technique, particularly as the thematic coherence of the individual voice parts is sufficient to offset the reduced degree of tonal stability in chromatic or twelve-note harmony. The series is also most naturally disposed in horizontally moving parts and retains its aural identity far more successfully than when disposed vertically in chordal passages. Many old contrapuntal devices of the Renaissance and Baroque epochs have been revived, though these well defined polyphonic forms are now tending to fall into disuse in favour of free contrapuntal writing. However, serialism has certainly brought in yet another major polyphonic epoch and in the hands of some composers, contrapuntal forms have become the medium for highly poetic expressions. One of the most lyrical of serial composers—Luigi Dallapiccola—is also one who has made most use of conventional canonic forms.

CONVENTIONAL CONTRAPUNTAL FORMS

Polyphony literally means music of 'many sounds' and results from the combination of two or more melodic strands which, though apparently independent, fit together to make musical sense. The melodic strands may be loosely similar, especially in the note-groups which form the beginning of the most characteristic phrases. This is called 'imitation'. If the melodic strands are identical throughout, even though transposed, inverted or in retrograde, we call this 'canon'. If the parts are dissimilar, this is 'free counterpoint'. Counterpoint is the art of combining melodies, but the term has also the more academic meaning of the science and technique of writing polyphonic music.

Some aspects of traditional contrapuntal usages have no application in serial composition. Indeed the study of 'species' and 16th-century 'strict counterpoint' was designed for musical circumstances which have ceased to exist (though their study can be an excellent, though pedantic, preparatory discipline). It is the old technique of canon which has best served serial composers and a study of this subject is essential both as a discipline and as a means of mastering a valuable and effective musical form.

The most simple form of canon is that in two parts at the unison:

(Two-part canon at the unison)

As will be seen, the following voice or 'consequent' is identical to the leading voice or 'antecedent'. In conventional canon, the consequent usually follows the antecedent at a regular metrical distance, so that normally it would begin after the first beat in bar two (or after the third beat in bar one). However, in serial music, excessive metrical regularity can be undesirable, so we have chosen to begin the consequent after an irregular metrical interval of only three beats, rather than after two or four beats. In this way, musical events which occur on the strong beats in the antecedent fall on weak beats in the consequent and *vice versa*, thus tending to form interesting rhythmical irregularities.

Though this canon at the unison works perfectly well (and also if the consequent is transposed up or down an octave) the result is not completely satisfactory. The repetition of the same notes in the following voice so soon after those of the leading voice causes them to lose freshness, so that the general effect can be dull and a little over-obvious. In order to eliminate this 'note fatigue', it is usual to transpose the consequent so that each note is endowed with a new interest:

(Two-part canon with transposed consequent)

In transposing the consequent, there is no need to follow conventional practice and use only transpositions to related tonalities at the fourth or fifth above or below the leading voice. Indeed such procedures, if they really have tonal significance, would be better avoided. It is sometimes best also to avoid transposition one tone lower, as this can produce a sense of depression. Transpositions to any other degree of the chromatic scale are good, but those at a third or sixth seem the strongest, while transpositions at the tritone seem most calculated to have a tonality-obscuring effect.

(All the examples in this chapter have been written with the series for Webern's Songs, Op. 23, with its 'I', 'R', and 'RI' versions as shown in Exx. 27–30.)

INVERSIONS

In canon by inversion, an upward moving interval in the antecedent becomes a downward interval in the consequent and *vice versa*. If the leading voice uses the 'O' or 'R' version of the series, the following voice will use the 'I' or 'RI' versions. Canon by inversion has a more subtle interest than canon at the unison or by transposition, which by comparison are a little over-obvious. Canon by inversion is naturally more difficult to follow; in fact what it gains in intellectual appeal can easily be lost by lack of audible coherence. However, as the resulting enigmatic quality has been much preferred by serial composers to contrapuntal expressions of a more obvious and easily-perceived nature, we find that canon by inversion has been used very frequently.

An inverted consequent may be transposed to any suitable position, in fact all transpositions are equally good as long as octaves do not occur and the resultant interval tensions are satisfactory. In the following example, using the same antecedent as previously, the 'I' version beginning on F cannot be used for the consequent, as octaves occur at F♯ in bar two. Similarly all other transpositions except those beginning in G♯, A or B♭ produce undesirable defects. Of these, the 'I' version beginning on G♯ seems to be the most suitable:

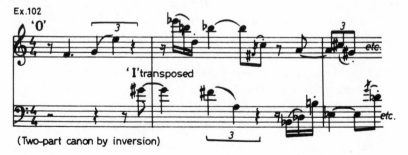

Ex.102

(Two-part canon by inversion)

We must note that the difficulty in finding a suitable transposed 'I' version for this new (inverted) consequent originates from the fact that the antecedent already exists and cannot be modified. Indeed it is very unlikely that a consequent can be successfully written for an antecedent which already exists in its entirety and cannot be altered. In writing canon, it is therefore essential to write both antecedent and consequent(s) together, as the movement of the leading voice determines everything that happens in those that follow. It is the antecedent which must suit the consequents and not *vice versa*.

CANON IN THREE OR MORE PARTS

In traditional canonic structures of three or more parts, it was quite common to introduce the consequents at regular metrical distances and without any transposition except that of register. The introduction of following voices at irregular distances and transpositions into any other key than the dominant were regarded as factors tending to detract from the logic and comprehensibility of the structure, rather than contribute an added interest. We therefore find such canons as that in the finale of Geminiani's Concerto Grosso in G minor Op. 3 No. 2, in which four voices follow each other at one-bar intervals, and without anything but octave transposition. By this very rhythmic regularity, constructional symmetry and singleness of tonality, the music has a noble vitality and supreme clarity.

Unfortunately, in serial music, canons revealing such symmetrical design and absence of transposition tend to lack interest, firstly because rhythmic regularity creates monotony by virtue of the lack of rhythmic contrast, secondly because the absence of transposition creates note fatigue, with a consequent decrease in interest in the notes of the following voices both in their melodic and harmonic values.

This is why canons in serial music (and those in any highly chromatic writing) of three or more parts usually demonstrate features designed to remove excessive rhythmic regularity and tonal and melodic stagnation. In the following example of a three-part canon, two kinds of rhythmic and metrical irregularity have been used. Firstly, the lower voice enters at a distance of three beats, thus going against the metrical structure (4/4) which would normally require the consequent to begin after an even number of beats. This causes *metrical displacement*. Secondly, the upper voice enters after one and a half beats, so that the rhythmic accentuations of the leading voice are displaced. All 'on the beat' accentuations become 'off beat' and all 'off beat' accentuations fall on the beat. This causes *rhythmic displacement*:

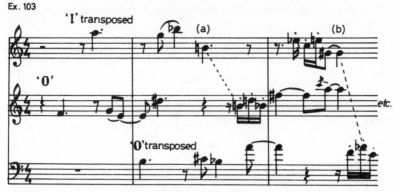

(Three-part canon, with one consequent inverted.)

Even greater rhythmic displacements could be introduced by beginning voices on the second or fourth semiquavers of a beat. Rhythmic displacement is even more effective than metrical displacement and especially in music which moves with a strong metrical pulse, can produce very attractive and subtle effects.

In this example tonal and melodic stagnation has been avoided by using a transposed inverted consequent in the upper voice and a tritone transposition in the lower. Where the same note occurs simultaneously in two parts it is kept at the unison as at (a) in bar two and (b) in bar three.

CANON CANCRIZANS, DIMINUTIONS, AND AUGMENTATIONS

In the canon cancrizans, retrograde or 'crab' canon, the imitating voice gives out the melody backwards, so that both voices usually begin together and end together:

Ex.104

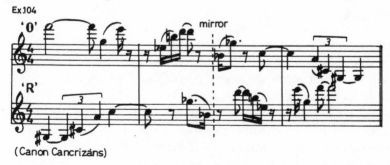

(Canon Cancrizáns)

At the halfway point the two parts naturally 'mirror' each other and due to the similarity of notes and rhythmic movement at the mirror, stagnation can easily occur. Apart from care at the mirror it is important that musically, the retrograde is just as interesting as the original. Usually this calls for special care in the rhythmic aspect of the retrograde.

Sometimes the imitating voice is displaced to begin before or after the original, in order to introduce metrical displacement:

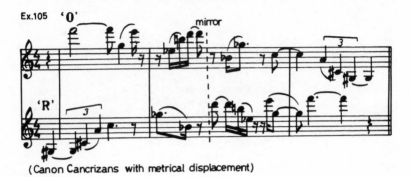

(Canon Cancrizans with metrical displacement)

Not infrequently in canon cancrizans, the leading voice is heard alone until the mirror point. It then procedes in retrograde, accompanied by an imitating voice which uses only the original or 'forward-moving' section. This is best illustrated in the following design:

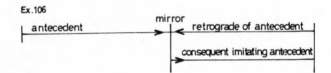

An illustration of such a retrograde canon by Dallapiccola has been given in Ex. 64, though it will be noticed that the imitating voice is displaced, beginning before the mirror point. This displacement is not infrequent in such structures.

So far we have dealt only with canon cancrizans in two parts. Such canons can be accompanied by one or more free voices, or by other parts using a different canonic form. Double canon cancrizans are possible, but rare. Quite frequently, however, a retrograde canon is accompanied by a diminished or augmented version of the antecedent. For instance, the canon cancrizans used for our illustrations may be accompanied by a transposed version of the antecedent *diminished* to half the original time values, so that it begins at the 'mirror' and proceeds to the end at double speed:

94

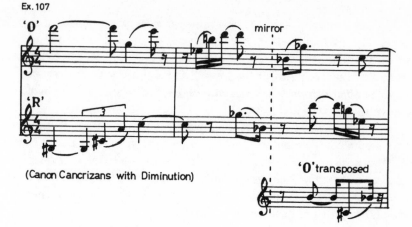

Ex. 107

(Canon Cancrizans with Diminution)

As, in canon by *augmentation*, the augmented voice may be considerably longer than the antecedent, this latter is usually repeated either in normal or retrograde form. In fact the design shown in Ex. 106 could be altered to include an augmented consequent as follows:

Ex.108

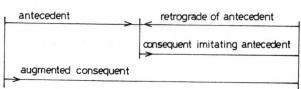

Naturally, if we do not wish the augmented consequent to begin and end on the same notes as the other parts, it would have to be transposed.

DOUBLE CANON

In double canon, there are two different two-part canons at the same time. The two antecedents need not start together, in fact one usually serves as accompaniment to the other, so that the principal antecedent and its consequent are heard in the foreground and the secondary canon can serve as a background. Two examples, by Stravinsky and Webern, are shown in Exx. 127 and 134.

In actual practice composers usually treat canonic or other contrapuntal forms with considerable freedom, in order to achieve more poetic results. There is no artistic value in pursuing abstruse canons to their ultimate conclusion, if that conclusion is in reality a 'bitter end'. We often find therefore that composers frequently start canons but avoid their completion, the reason being that to bring such musical sections to a satisfactory close, free part-writing is often indispensable. In canonic practice, there is a great wisdom in knowing when to stop!

The more conventional contrapuntal forms have, however, given way to freer contrapuntal styles, some of which will now be illustrated:

RHYTHMIC COUNTERPOINTS AND CANONS

A counterpoint or canon may be imitated in its *rhythmic* aspect only, ignoring the intervallic sequence of the original notes and reproducing only the rhythmic configuration. For instance, the antecedent of the two-part canon in Ex. 100 may be accompanied by a consequent which imitates the rhythm of the leading voice, but not the intervals:

Ex.109

(Rhythmic Canon)

This produces a *rhythmic canon*. The same procedure can be used with any kind of imitation and in any number of parts. Naturally this device avoids the sense of mechanical repetition which real imitation or canon can produce.

FREE COUNTERPOINTS

Free counterpoints usually avoid any repetition between the various parts, in fact the voices are usually made up of differing rhythmic designs. In the following example, the antecedent of Ex. 100 is accompanied by a free voice using contrasting rhythms:

(Free Counterpoint)

This process is frequently carried a stage further by the *free numbering of parts*, that is, each horizontal 'voice' is not made up of a sucession of single sounds, but is formed by vertical combinations of various numbers of notes. In the following example, using the same rhythms as in the previous illustration, each voice contains combinations of one, two, and three-note chords:

Ex.111

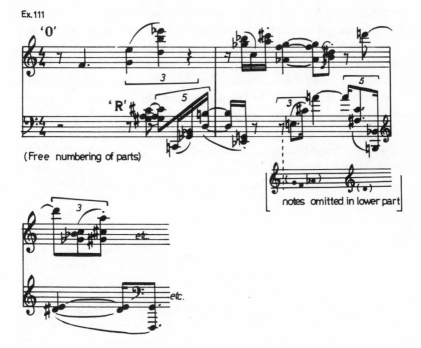

(Free numbering of parts)

notes omitted in lower part

This kind of contrapuntal writing is particularly suited to keyboard compositions, but is frequently adapted for orchestral use. In working the above example, the 'O' and 'R' versions of the series for Webern's Op. 23 has again been used and certain omissions from the 'R' version (lower voice) have been inevitable, as noted on the lowest stave. These omissions (G, F, A♭, and D) have been necessary in order to eliminate octaves with the upper part. The omitted notes could have been included in the lower stave as soon after as possible, but this has not been done in order to maintain a freer circulation of the total chromatic and thus avoid any possibility of note fatigue.

PROPORTIONALISMS

Contrapuntal writing using numerical proportions and rhythmic proportions is not uncommon in serial music and is fully dealt with in Chapter 15.

MIRROR FORMS AND STRUCTURES

Quite apart from retrograde canons, where the voices are built around a 'mirror', serial music is frequently written in mirror forms and structures (sometimes called 'palindromes') which may be formed from loosely imitative counterpoint, or any kind of free counterpoint. Indeed mirror structures need not necessarily be contrapuntal at all, but these non-contrapuntal types will be dealt with later in Chapter 10 on Forms. For the time being it is sufficient to observe that any polyphonic music may be made into a mirror structure, or into a succession of mirrored sections which combine to form a complete movement. For instance, in Webern's Variations Op. 27 for piano the first movement is made up of fourteen short mirror structures. The last movement also contains true mirror sections and also 'rhythmic mirrors' where only the rhythms and not the notes are mirrored. Indeed, in the first movement, Webern pursues the technique of 'mirroring' to its utmost limits. As the following example shows, not only is the seven-bar section mirrored at the half-way point (bar 40), but the note-orders are mirrored and also the number of notes played by each hand:

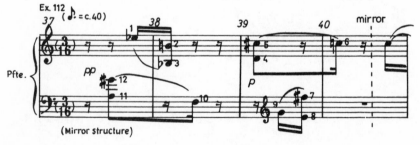

Webern: *Variations for Piano*, Op.27

98

In the first two bars the right hand plays one note followed by two, while the left plays two followed by one. This process continues throughout the whole section—whatever the right hand does, the left then reproduces in retrograde. Furthermore, the vertical note-order of the series is rigorously mirrored—the 'upward' order 12 and 11 in the left hand (first bar) is reversed by the 'downward' order 2 and 3 in the right (second bar). This order is then reversed in the third bar. Even the rests seem to follow a mirror pattern. It would seem that Webern has tried to produce mirrors of every musical factor, even if many of these structural details can have no real audible significance.

However, the *general* aspects of these mirror sections are quite easily discernable to the listener, which is more than can be said for many other mirror structures, especially those which form large musical sections. For instance, Luigi Nono uses a mirror plan in two works (*Varianti* and *Composizione* for orchestra) which can have virtually no audible significance. Both works comprise the exposition of two long sections and then the same sections played in retrograde (Section A—Section B—A retrograde—B retrograde). As both *Varianti* and *Composizione* last about a quarter of an hour, it would seem virtually impossible to associate any section with its mirror and therefore the musical value of these forms is open to question. Such structures could certainly be an excellent means of writing twice as much music with little more effort, their logic as 'paper method' is beyond question, but we must make sure that such mirroring does not result in music of dubious *audible* merit. If mirror forms are used, we must be sure that the process produces positive musical results and that poetic values are never sacrificed for hypothetical intellectual concepts.

INTELLIGIBILITY

This brings us to the whole question of the intelligibility or otherwise of serial music in polyphonic styles. In previous polyphonic epochs, the contrapuntal associations between one voice and another were usually fairly evident. The clearer the association, the more positive the value of the contrapuntal usage. In general, the clarity of contrapuntal discourse was therefore cultivated to a considerable degree and certainly not shunned as an undesirable element.

On the other hand, in serial music of contrapuntal types, the reverse is probably more true. Composers have seemed to avoid contrapuntal clarity rather than cultivate it. The reasons are not completely clear, but we can be sure that when the creative minds of a whole artistic movement tend towards the same practice, there must be some very valid aesthetic justification for their actions. One reason has already been hinted at several times—that is, that when imitation is too evident in serial music, the result is a little over-obvious, mechanical, and lacking in subtlety. The intellectual appeal of clear contrapuntal associations is mysteriously dispelled, the magic facade of lucid polyphony for some obscure reason loses much of its allure. This is a strange paradox, for one would expect clarity of contrapuntal associations to have even more positive value in music of obscure tonal relationships than when the tonal discourse was completely unambiguous.

Another reason, but only of a secondary nature, is that of stylistic change. Atonalism and serialism belong to revolutionary movements in opposition to many of the tenets of classicism and neo-classicism, so inevitably the characteristic clarity of discourse in these latter tended to be eliminated purely on stylistic grounds. However, this is not the end of the story. We know that many revolutionary ideas have not always permanent, universal values, in which case they fall into disuse. But today the tendency to avoid obvious contrapuntal associations is even greater than at the time of the atonal and serial revolutions. This can only mean that we are dealing with a phenomenon which has not the impermanency of a revolutionary slogan, but the permanency of a genuine artistic means of expression, part and parcel of an artist's way of speaking to the age in which he lives.

Contrapuntal indefinition must therefore be an element of positive value in today's musical language. It is a contributing factor towards that enigmatic, indeterminate, subtle, recondite, esoteric, transcendental form of self-expression which in music and all the arts is spreading from Tokyo to San Francisco, from Stockholm to Wellington, N.Z. We are free to follow the same path or not, just as we like; there is no obligation. But, before closing this chapter, there is one observation to make. It is becoming more and more easy to be enigmatic and obscure (in polyphony or otherwise): the techniques for such a language are fully developed. But it is becoming more and more difficult to achieve a *satisfactory lucidity*. This may well be our next task, but only the future can decide.

10. FORMS

Definition of Form. Principles of Form. Classical Forms. Variation Forms. Perpetual Variation. Ostinato. Contrapuntal Forms. Vocal Forms. Mirror Structures or Palindromes. Free Forms. Predetermined Forms. Forms Resulting from Improvisation.

DEFINITION OF FORM

Before describing the various musical forms which are suitable to serial music, it is important to stress that forms are by no means well-compartmented, standardized moulds into which a composer only needs to pour his musical ideas in order to obtain an end-product of perfect shape and structure. If such ready-made moulds were used, the results would have the monotonous uniformity of plastic toys and be just about as interesting.

Unfortunately, the conception of form as being a pre-conceived framework which from the outset determines the shape of the music is all too prevalent. In reality the reverse is probably more true—that form is the resultant shape created by the composer's sculpturing of his musical conceptions. Musical forms have always been created through the shaping and developing of musical ideas, they have never been invented as abstract formulas to which musical ideas must be made to conform. If they have, the results have not been conspicuously successful.

In actual practice it is best to regard 'form' as having a dual significance, both as a noun—the musical 'shape' which outwardly confines the composer's thoughts, and as a verb—the process of forming and sculpturing musical ideas into a convincing whole. This latter conception of form—as an act rather than as a fact—seems to have particular relevance in serial music. For the old classical forms have not proved completely suitable to atonal idioms and have tended to give way to music which is exclusively the result of the 'act' of forming. In some ways we can draw an analogy with the visual arts. The old classical musical forms may be likened to representational painting or sculpture in which the artist uses visual forms (more or less freely) as vehicles for his self-expression. Serial music may be likened to more recent non-representational art which is the product of the artist's untrammelled imagination, even in some cases (e.g. action painting) resulting from the physical act of working.

PRINCIPLES OF FORM

However, the really basic principles of form remain unchanged. For the act of 'forming' music still remains what it has always been—a process designed to captivate the listener's attention, to hold it continuously to the end and to leave him with a sense of having experienced something complete and inevitable. All good music satisfies these three fundamental requirements—to arouse interest, to maintain it, and when the music has run its course to leave an impression of completeness and fulfilment.

The very history of the development of musical forms reveals the composer's continuous efforts to keep these principles alive, and reconcile them with the developing potentialities of his audiences. At first music built on a single idea (or *unitary* form) was sufficient, but movements were inevitably brief. In an effort to meet the demand for longer movements, yet avoid monotony, a second theme or idea was introduced. Then repetition with decoration was resorted to. As the experience of listeners developed, so did the principles of development and variation until sonata, rondo, and variation forms could be successfully built which sustained interest over considerable periods. But throughout this period of formal growth, it was the second of our principles—that of maintaining interest—which created so much difficulty. It is easy enough to arouse interest at the beginning of a twenty-minute movement, but a herculean task to keep it going. And as the same is still true, we might consider for a moment how past composers overcame the problem and see how it applies today.

The problem of maintaining interest was overcome by avoiding both the monotony of excessive repetition and the fatigue of absorbing too much new material. No audience can keep awake through the eternal reiteration of a single idea. Nor can the human mind withstand a continuous bombardment of new ideas. Composers had to strike a perfect balance between the extreme poles of perpetual change and perpetual repetition—new material was only introduced at the psychological point of complete attunement with the old. Once the new material had run its course, the mind was rested by a welcome return to the already-familiar. Soon it was ready again to grasp new ideas, so some new subject-matter was introduced, or the old material subjected to adventurous changes, until the old themes could re-emerge with welcome freshness. This happy mean between change and repetition is the fundamental basis of so many sonata and rondo movements. It is also the basis of a great deal of serial music, though the repetitions are usually skilfully disguised.

Audiences change, their potentialities develop and their needs undergo considerable mutation. Today our minds are attuned to a considerably greater degree of change than any audience of only fifty years ago. Not only do we find repetition correspondingly less necessary, but it can so easily smack of the rhetorical that, often enough, we prefer to do without it.

However, though much music would seem already to presume that we are ready to digest new ideas in almost every moment, indeed to be *startled* in every bar, this is probably not the case. The real truth is that at a certain point, the human mind, against our own volition, erects a barrier and refuses to digest any more novelties, declines to be startled and just goes to sleep. This is why, though it is fashionable enough to create music of perpetual novelty, it would be wiser to retain just a modicum of the age-old balance by salting the 'new' with a pinch of the 'old'. This by no means signifies that the 'old' need be mentioned in its original form. It may be sufficient just to make a passing suggestion of its mood—no more. The important thing is that the human mind may be refreshed and re-orientated by a suggestion of something once-heard, that it finds a footing before being swept along the turbulent course of new events.

Other principles of form we must observe are also old enough, though they may present themselves in a new guise. The emotional scale of the music must be in proportion to the size of the work. The emotional gamut of a brief piece of chamber music must be comparatively limited, that of an extended orchestral work must surge over a large span. Themes or ideas must be proportionate in strength to the length of course they have to run. Subsidiary sections should not overshadow principal sections. Points of tension, climax, and repose should be strategically placed. There must be a perfect proportioning of principal and subsidiary parts, contrasts of colour and texture between the various sections, moments of preparation and of fulfilment. In spite of extreme variety we must preserve indisputable unity —but not uniformity. All these are important factors, but subsidiary to our three main formal requirements. As in the difficult art of short-story writing, we must above all arouse interest and a sympathetic hearing, maintain it, and round it off into a convincing and satisfying whole.

We will now turn to discussion of the various form-types available, beginning with those most closely related to tradition.

CLASSICAL FORMS

Some classical forms are based so essentially on a limited amount of thematic material, coupled with elaborations based largely on key contrasts, that they are of little practical value in serial music. These are unitary forms, simple binary and simple ternary forms, and fugue.

Other forms such as sonata and rondo, which are able to support a considerable diversity of thematic material and elaboration, have been frequently used by serial composers. Sometimes the classical phrase-forming techniques are in evidence, sometimes not. But invariably there is no attempt to follow the classical tonal schemes, which are by no means necessary in more complex usage of these forms. Most frequently the recapitulation, or repetition of themes is abbreviated or disguised, for themes are often inverted or further elaborated. Sometimes such forms may fall into a pattern of the exposition of various ideas, followed by transformations and elaborations which rarely, if ever, re-present ideas in their original form, yet the basic design behind the whole scheme may be completely classical. In fact many serial compositions belong to this category, without the composers being aware that in reality they have followed traditional principles to a considerable extent.

VARIATION FORMS

In the old 'air with variations', the main element of variation was usually confined to thematic elaboration. The melody was used as a skeleton framework for successive types of decoration, while the harmonic background and metrical structure remained unaltered.

However, in serial music, such variation-types are conspicuously absent. The term 'variation' is used in a looser sense, referring to the elaboration of a certain amount of 'material' or often enough, of the series itself. But such serial variations fall into two main types—those which create a succession of short movements, each of distinct and clear-cut character, and those which do not, but create constantly changing music based on the principle of 'perpetual variation'. For the moment we are not concerned with perpetual variation which will be dealt with separately.

The serial variations which create successions of short, distinct movements are again of various types. The variations may follow each other without a break to form a large movement. For instance, Schoenberg's Variations for Orchestra, Op. 31 consists of an introduction, a theme, nine variations of various durations, and a finale comprising three different sections, all played continuously to form an extended work of over five hundred bars. There is a degree of thematic unity in the work, especially through the use of the motto theme BACH.

The finale of Webern's Symphony Op. 21 is again a continuous movement comprising theme, seven variations, and coda, but there are no thematic relationships between variations and theme. The only connection is one of structure. As shown in Ex. 79, the theme is a rhythmic mirror of eleven bars' duration and each variation and the coda is built on the same eleven-bar mirror principle.

On the other hand, some variations consist of a succession of separate movements, each complete in itself, with a fair degree of contrast of mood and texture between the movements. A good example is Dallapiccola's

Variations for Orchestra,[1] which consists of eleven movements. These comprise canonic and contrapuntal pieces interspersed by characteristic pieces entitled 'Accents', 'Lines', 'Rhythms', 'Colours', 'Shadows', etc. Each piece is fairly brief, the longest being less than three minutes' duration. Though certain melodic fragments are common between occasional movements, in reality these variations comprise completely independent and self-contained pieces, with no element in common except that they are based on the same series.

However, the important factor to establish in these types of variations is that whether the music is continuous or separated into isolated movements, there is always a complete constancy of character within each variation. Once a certain musical design or mood has been established, this is not abandoned until the whole variation is complete.

PERPETUAL VARIATION

In perpetual variation the concept of creating a succession of well-defined, self-contained and contrasting sections is abandoned. From the outset, the composer's principle is that of the continuous mutation and elaboration of a given quantity of 'material'. Naturally the overall pattern created falls outside any classical formal design and belongs to the realm of 'free' forms, the main principles of which will be discussed later.

OSTINATO

In classical music, a continuously repeated musical phrase was often used as foundation material, over which was constructed music of considerable variety of texture and mood. This 'ostinato' served as a unifying force in many pieces of grandiose proportions, and though continuous repetition is largely avoided today, we can still find occasional examples of music where the underlying unity is provided by some form of ostinato. This may take the form of the repetition of a small group of notes, of a rhythm, or merely some recurring colouristic effect. The ostinato design may be subjected to considerable change, or it may only recur at intervals. The passage may only be a brief interpolation in a larger structure. But in spite of its seeming limitations, the form is still evident in Webern's music if not in that of his successors.

CONTRAPUNTAL FORMS

Polyphonic forms have been fully dealt with in our previous chapter. It only remains for us to make a single observation, that is, that contrapuntal forms need not be always used in isolation, in separate compartments, but may be interwoven into the pattern of larger movements either as major episodes or merely as subsidiary sections.

[1]Dallapiccola's Variations for Orchestra is an orchestrated version of his *Quaderno Musicale di Annalibera* for piano, already mentioned (cf. Exx. 11 and 59).

In vocal music the form has always depended on the relative degree of importance the composer has wished to give to words or music. Ever since renaissance times the same problem has existed—should the words be made to fit into an independent musical mould, or should the music be a servant to the drama of the words and take its form only from them?

Today the divergence of ideas seems greater than ever before. On the one hand we find Stravinsky willing to adopt the contemplative, passive attitude of the renaissance composers, using archaic polyphonic and homophonic vocal forms with seeming indifference to the emotive flow of the text. On the other we have composers such as Dallapiccola, Berio, or Boulez, wringing the last ounce of drama from the words and letting them dominate the musical form.

This is no place to discuss the rights or wrongs of either faction, all we must observe is that both sides have their reasons which are perfectly valid in given situations. In actual practice, in serial music we find that choral pieces, for practical reasons, are frequently written using archaic choral forms, whereas music for solo voice is usually more dramatic, with its formal shape determined by the poetic text alone. This subject is more fully developed in our chapter on vocal writing. It only remains at this point to observe that there is a great danger in relying too much in formal matters on the poetic text, firstly because words are so often indistinguishable, secondly because the result may easily be musically inconclusive. A spoken poem may be formally perfect, yet when it is spread over a larger time-span (as inevitably happens in a musical setting) and the metrical design distorted, the poem's formal plan may be completely destroyed and no amount of dramatic or lyrical word-painting can save the result from resembling a frenetic display of empty histrionics. It is the *musical* value of vocal music which in the end is of paramount importance and therefore the dictates of musical form must not be ignored.

MIRROR STRUCTURES OR PALINDROMES

The Greek word *palindromos* literally means 'running back', and usually refers to a word, verse, or sentence that reads the same backwards and forward, such as *madam*. Musically, palindromes are similar to the mirror forms we have discussed in our previous chapter, except that they are not necessarily of a contrapuntal nature. Palindromes are usually large mirror structures, often spanning a whole movement, in which the second half is an exact mirror of the first part. Alternatively, a large movement may comprise a number of palindromes of various lengths and characters.

There are a number of ways of modifying this scheme, to produce more subtle results which we may call 'free palindromes'. These are:

1. The palindrome may be one in which the note-order only is mirrored. That is, the second half mirrors the note-order of the first, but the rhythmic configuration is completely changed.

2. The rhythmic structure of the palindrome may be mirrored, but all note-orders may be altered.

3. A true palindrome may be used in conjunction with other parts which follow a different formal design. This scheme is particularly useful if the palindrome is used only as an accompanimental feature, subsidiary to a principal musical design, or an independent melody.

Inevitably, in all palindrome structures, we must be sure that all mirroring sections have the same vitality and musical value as the 'forward-going' sections. We must beware that mirroring is no mechanical procedure, but a means of creating valid expressions, particularly as the formal design of palindromes remains audibly imperceptible.

FREE FORMS

Music of 'free form' comes nearest of all to that conception of form as the 'act of forming' we referred to at the beginning of this chapter. The shape of the music is not determined by any conventional (or unconventional) overall structure.[2] It is the result of one factor only—the composer's moulding and sculpturing of sound—material into a shape which corresponds with the course of his emotive thought. *Free forms must follow an emotive path*. All too often, they are regarded as mere abstractions, devoid of any progression of interior emotive impulses. If this were really so, the music would not only be formally negative, but void of any humanistic expression and therefore worthless.

We must therefore beware of regarding free forms as abstract expressions, but think of them rather as positive means of conveying human emotions. They must be forms 'in movement', charged with emotive impetus and running the whole gamut of human feelings.

To use free forms successfully, certain principles must be observed and certain pitfalls avoided. The main trap into which it is so easy to fall is that of writing short-breathed musical phrases which surge frenetically over a large emotional span in a brief period of time. All possibility of continuity of emotion is therefore eliminated, the listener is quickly disorientated and his attention wanes. Furthermore, as the music runs the whole emotional gamut in a brief spell, extended movements cannot be successfully written.

---

[2]Inevitably there is a complete absence of repetition in melodic shapes and rhythmic designs, as any form of repetition would be the first step towards conventional formal constructions.

In using free forms it is therefore important to build a whole work on a preconceived plan of emotive tension values. Each movement and sub-section will then have a specific contribution to the overall emotive plan. There will be adequate periods of tension and repose. Climaxes will be prepared and sustained, they will be graduated according to their importance in the overall design and will be followed by adequate periods of tension-decline.

In using free forms, composers usually take care to divide the music into fairly well-defined periods, usually characterized by special effects of tempo, texture, or tone colour. Thus to some extent the work is sectionalized into a specific succession of events, each spanning an adequate time-space. Too-frequent and excessive changes of tempo, texture and tone colour are usually avoided, otherwise there is a danger of a haphazard, incoherent result which borders on formlessness. An example of the division of a work into well-defined sections is to be found in Luciano Berio's *Serenata No. 1* for flute and fourteen instruments, which though performed in one continuous movement, is in reality subdivided as follows:

	bars	tempo
Flute solo (1)	1– 11	♪ = 60
Tutti (without flute)	12– 25	♪ = 60
Flute solo (2)	26– 32	♪ = 92
Flute, horn and strings	32– 56	♪ = 92
Flute, woodwind and brass	57– 62	♪ = 84
Flute, harp and piano	63– 73	♪ = 84
Flute, bass clarinet and strings	74– 94	♪ = 92 and 138
Flute and brass	95–102	♪ = 138
Flute, bass clarinet and strings	103–114	♪ = 138
Flute solo (3)	115–123	♪ = 138
Flute, harp, piano and woodwind	124–162	♪ = 84
Flute, harp, piano and strings	163–168	♪ = 84
Tutti with flute	169–188	♪ = 84 and 60
Tutti without flute	189–215	♪ = 92 and 84
Tutti with flute	216–226	♪ = 92 and 60
Flute solo (4) cadenza	227–240	♪ = 92
Flute, woodwind, harp and piano	241–258	♪ = 92

In order to present such a clear-cut plan, some simplification has been resorted to (for example, in the first tutti (without flute), the flute plays a few notes, but as they cover only two quavers out of thirteen bars, they have been disregarded). But the above subdivision gives a fairly faithful representation of the main course of events. It will be seen that the flute plays solo in four sections and that the full tutti is also used in four sections, twice with the flute and twice without. In all other parts the flute is accompanied either by each instrumental group alone (i.e. woodwind, brass, strings, or harp and piano) or by various combinations of these groups. At first the accompaniment combinations are more straightforward than those used later on. But usually, once the accompanimental group has been chosen, it is not changed over an adequate time period. Similarly, though numerous changes of tempo occur, each tempo lasts for an adequate duration and is chosen from a fixed range of five possible speeds (= 60, 84, 92, 108, and 138). Tempo changes often coincide with changes of instrumental combinations, but tend to remain unchanged over longer spans at first than in the last third of the work. At the same time, the general mood of each section is constant. One section may remain calm, another will be agitated. The flute plays one solo in a lyrical vein, in another it is quietly subdued, while in the final cadenza it pursues a wild, vertiginous course in an atmosphere of thrilling excitement.

However, the listener is not aware of the sectional division of the work. One musical section merges well with the next, there is a sense of unity and not diversity, as *the emotive continuity of the music is never interrupted.*

It is quite evident that with free forms each work will have its own formal problem, to be solved in its own unique way, so that to lay down precise rules would not only be impractical but completely wrong. The composer's problem is to provide both unity and diversity, to balance adequate constancy with adequate change, and to lead the listener along a coherent path of emotive impressions.

Free forms inevitably call for a virtuoso use of all factors which contribute to those 'emotive tension values' already described in our chapter on writing melody (see 'Formal design in melody', Chapter 5). The factors there described which contribute to tension and relaxation in melody are precisely the same as those to be used in music of many parts and to these may be added the rich resources of harmony, texture, and tone colour. These latter, however, are only secondary values, serving to intensify and adequately clothe the primary factors in the time—movement, pitch, and volume dimensions.

We again summarize those factors which tend to create tension and relaxation in music:

TENSION

Rapid movement
Increasing impetus   (Time/movement
Strong metrical pulse   dimension)
Irregular rhythms, well defined

Maximum height or depth   (Pitch dimension)
Strong melodic intervals

Maximum volume
Contrasting silence
Virile dynamics and strong dynamic contrasts   (Volume dimension)
Staccato phrasing

Harsh harmony

Complex textures

Virile tone colours

RELAXATION

Tranquil movement
Declining impetus   (Time/movement
Weak or indeterminate metrical pulse   dimension)
Flowing rhythms, or 'vague' rhythms

Avoidance of extreme registers   (Pitch dimension)
Weaker melodic intervals

Quiet dynamics
Non-contrasting silence
Reduced dynamic contrasts   (Volume dimension)
Legato phrasing

Smooth harmony

Thin, simple textures

Mellow tone colours

Naturally, in the above list of factors which contribute towards tension and relaxation, each has been considered in isolation. But in actual practice, tense and relaxed qualities frequently coexist. For instance, there are innumerable contexts where tense qualities in the time-movement dimension are coupled with relaxed qualities in the volume dimension (e.g. rapid movement and strong metrical pulse, coupled with quiet dynamics and legato phrasing). In fact there is very frequently, in much serial music, a continuous *interaction* of all these factors, with results of considerable complexity. It is precisely this interaction of various factors which allows infinite gradations of tense and relaxed qualities. The difficulty of assessing complex relationships of the various factors which create tension and relaxation may lead us to judge the total effect purely subjectively. But in free forms, where these factors are very essential means of giving coherent shape to the music, it is particularly important to learn to assess every effect and to estimate carefully the total result of combinations of various factors. Any composer who shirks this task belongs to that class of composers who do not know what their music sounds like until after it is played.

These tension and relaxation factors are equally applicable in any kind of serial music, or in free twelve-note composition, for their values are constant in any non-tonal situation.

PRE-DETERMINED FORMS

These forms result from the formation of structures built on principles of integral serialism and proportionalisms which will be discussed in Chapter 15. It is premature to go into questions of method here. For the moment we will limit our observations to one single factor—that the musical form can either determine the kind of construction used, or it can be the result of a certain system of structure. The form can therefore be the dominant factor which determines all other principles of construction, or it can be the resultant product of the method.

FORMS RESULTING FROM IMPROVISATION

Improvisation (discussed in Chapter 15) is usually based on some skeleton design. Sometimes the performer has a completely free choice in formal matters, at others he has to improvise in turn on various musical patterns which may have to follow each other in strict order, or which he can order as he wishes. On first thoughts it would seem that only very haphazard forms can result. But in ideal conditions a good performer will create coherent emotive patterns closely allied to those produced in 'free forms'. Good improvisation is an excellent example of that 'act of forming' which should underlie our approach to form even in compositions of more calculated structure, if our work is to have vitality, impetus, and emotive strength.

II. VOCAL WRITING

Writing for Solo Voice. Technical Points. Choral Music.

WRITING FOR SOLO VOICE

It is symptomatic of the multiplicity of artistic movements of this century that while some composers were not only rediscovering and publishing the old folk-songs, but even composing imitations of them, others were writing vocal music which led to a complete break with traditional song-writing. These latter composers have mostly been the Viennese School and their successors.

Before reviewing their work, it will not be amiss to consider for a moment just what traditional song means, and therefore just what the 'break with tradition' signifies. Apart from the obvious facts that traditional songs have always been composed in well-defined tonal frameworks, that phrase constructions were usually symmetrical in shape, and that the 'memorable' quality of a melody depended on the repetition and evolution of basic phrase outlines, there is one important factor which is often insufficiently recognized—that is, that in traditional song, the music has had complete dominion over the words. Though we find exceptions in such composers as Wolf, with great classical song writers such as Schubert, it is the melody which is all-glorious. Though the melody and accompaniment may be exquisitely designed to express the general atmosphere of the words, the particular significance of each individual word is lost, overpowered by the commanding power of melody. Sufficient proof of this is that not only do we find the same musical phrases used for different words, but that many songs are strophic—the same music is repeated for a number of verses.

The only real exception has been in recitative and dramatic aria, where the significance and emotive power of individual words have been allowed to oust melody momentarily.

Serial composers have abandoned many of the principles of traditional song writers—tonal usage, symmetrical phrase constructions, and repetitions—but above all there has been an increasing tendency to dismantle the commanding edifice of melody and to build instead a structure in which music acts as a servant of the words, decorating them and intensifying their meaning without assuming a dominating role. Some composers lay great stress not only on the expressive power and significance of each word, but on the inherent musical qualities contained in the phonic structure of the word itself. Others devise a loosely lyrical melodic line which paints the emotions of the words. But the important factor is that melody of the old song and aria types has been largely abandoned, and for the moment we have a partial return to the ideals of the composers of the Florentine *Camerata*, who in turn sought to revive the old Greek declamation, with its emphasis on the expression of words.

The work which completely abandoned classical vocal styles and established the new declamatory manner was Schoenberg's *Pierrot Lunaire*, written as long ago as 1912. This is certainly an extremist work, for in this setting of twenty-one poems, the voice is hardly allowed to *sing* at all. Only fifteen notes are indicated as 'sung', all the rest is to be recited in *Sprechstimme* (i.e. 'speech voice'). Though for *Sprechstimme* the score indicates a definite pitch and rhythm for each syllable, the actual note indicated must be merely touched and not held as in singing. The intonation fluctuates between notes, with continuous crescendos and diminuendos of volume, so that an equilibrium between singing and natural speech is maintained. The following example from the third poem *(Der Dandy)* shows words recited in *Sprechstimme* (notes marked with a cross), followed by a final phrase which reverts to recitation at indefinite pitch:

Ex.113   Schoenberg: *Pierrot Lunaire*

und be-malt sein Ge-sicht in er-ha-be-nem Stil

mit ei-nem phan-ta-sti-chen Mond-strahl.

This manner of vocal writing is the chief contributing factor to that atmosphere of intense unreality and acute tension which make *Pierrot Lunaire* one of the most powerful of expressionist works.

In other works (e.g. *Ode to Napoleon Bonaparte* and *A Survivor from Warsaw*) Schoenberg continued to write for reciting voice, and the same means have been used to a smaller extent by Berg and Dallapiccola But these are cases of an extreme reversion to declamation. We have already quoted a few examples of vocal music which though departing from traditional vocal forms to some extent, still retain genuinely lyrical outlines, cf. Berg's *Song* (Ex. 2) and *Lied der Lulu* (Ex. 35), also Dallapiccola's *Il Prigioniero* (Ex. 4) and *Goethe-Lieder* (Ex. 64).

Today, the evidence would seem to be that while declamation is generally adhered to as a background 'form', composers make considerable efforts to expand it into a lyrical outline wherever possible:

Here it is quite obvious that as soon as the first section of declamation is disposed of, the composer has burst into a wide lyrical sweep on the final word.

In the following example from Boulez's *Improvisation sur Mallarmé No. 1* the composer has expanded the declamation into a vocal line which is almost of 'coloratura' shape, full of gentle nuances, decorations, and subtle inflections:

This is already a far cry both from tradition and from the rather mechanical *Sprechstimme* of *Pierrot Lunaire*. There is no doubt that though it is difficult to sing, it is eminently vocal music, and that while the words are given due importance, the purely musical effect is superb.

This unification of the poetic powers of words and music is powerfully created in Luciano Berio's *Circles*. Here the vocal line is not only strongly expressive, but each word seems to burst forth with full poetic power:

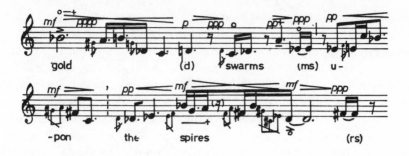

Though there is considerable decoration in the vocal line, with a lyrical expansiveness which is a true descendant of Italian *bel canto* tradition, each syllable is given prominence. The words are not hidden by the melody, but are cardinal points in the overall design. It would seem here that Schoenberg's abandonment of vocal tradition in *Pierrot Lunaire* has at last borne fruit of permanent artistic value.

TECHNICAL POINTS

Though it would be true to say that a vocal writer is born, not made, it is equally true that nowadays young composers with an inborn instinct for vocal composition still need to learn technique. It is no longer sufficient to have a tuneful mind, like so many songwriters of the past. Vocal writing has become a thing of skill as well as of instinct, and the best way to learn the trade is to see what other composers have done. The works of such composers as Luigi Dallapiccola will provide much more food for thought than what can be written here. However, for what they are worth, a few technical points are now given, as suggestions and aids, not as definite rules.

1. Melisma

Where words of greater poetic value occur, their emotive power can be enhanced by melisma. This means that the prominent vowel or vowels can be sung on a number of notes tied together in a musical phrase designed to enhance the lyrical expression (cf. the last two bars of Ex. 114).

2. Declamation

Unimportant words, or words of 'narrative' character can be declaimed. If they are declaimed in uniform rhythm and on the same note, the musical quality will be negative. Musical interest could only be introduced through a skilful accompaniment. On the other hand, disparate rhythms which suit the rhythmic pattern of the words, together with suitably rising and falling note-patterns will produce a more positive musical result.

3. Rhythms

Avoid obvious repetition of rhythms, if a non-traditional result is desired. Flexibility and contrast in rhythmic designs tend to introduce a lyrical quality, but as the melodic shapes have less definition than in repetitive designs, a certain vagueness of effect can result only too easily. The only way to combat this is to create impetus and contrasting decline in the rhythmic figuration at appropriate points in the text, so as constantly to renew interest.

Above all, avoid monotonous movement caused by successions of equal note values. Words have an individual rhythm of their own which is a far cry from the 'square' note patternings of tradition. The equal note values in classical song were dictated (and justified) by the metrical movement, which was such an essential melodic factor. This is no longer the case and today equal note-values sound merely inexpressive and rigid.

4. Accentuation of Words

Words should be stressed in proportion to their importance. Some should receive prominence, others should be subdued. Not all words should be equally accentuated, otherwise the vocal line will lack contour and the cardinal words of the poetry will remain submerged in the general pattern. To bring any word into prominence three things can be done. It can be set to the highest and longest note of a musical phrase, it can be given a stronger dynamic value than subordinate words, and it can be stressed by its position in the rhythmic design.

Conversely, subordinate words will be lower in pitch, of weaker dynamic values, and in less significant positions in the rhythmic design.

5. Dynamics

A traditional song or aria has usually few variations in dynamic volume and diminuendos or crescendos are usually gradual, lasting over a certain period. But in present-day vocal compositions, as in instrumental works, dynamics play a big role in the general expressive design. Changes of volume and style of attack are frequent and substantial, the atmosphere tending to be dramatic rather than passively contemplative (cf. Ex. 116).

6. Climaxes

Every poem will have its peak point of interest and probably also a number of less important ones. As these will coincide with the climax points of the music, it is best to reserve the maximum musical climax for the culminating word of the poetry and to distribute minor musical climax points among the subordinate peaks of poetical interest. It is advisable to reserve the highest note of a musical section for its point of climax. Just occasionally, the lowest note can also be used in this way, usually through an association of ideas. It would be quite in order to set words like 'deep', 'death' or 'grave' to the lowest note, especially if the general scale of volume is pianissimo, but otherwise high notes and loud dynamics are more characteristic of climax points.

7. *Decorations*

Grace notes and coloratura decorations can be used with good effect. Decorations can often include note repetitions, or the repetition of note-groups (see the repetitions of F♯ and E in the Boulez example just quoted). However, care should be taken that decorations have point, otherwise their over-use can destroy coherence. They are best used with the more poetic words, and not in passages of narrative.

8. *'Tone Painting'*

In traditional vocal music, the voice is used in a surprisingly limited way. Put crudely, it is used as a purveyor of vowel sounds interspersed by less desirable consonant noises. How often do we hear a singer who sings on one vowel only and subdues the consonants to such an extent that not one word is intelligible? Today vocal writers are exploiting a whole gamut of vocal sounds which tradition would have abhorred, but which in reality have a remarkable expressive power. These include not only the more obvious vocal effects such as whispering, humming, or 'non-vibrato', but the exploitation of consonant sounds of considerable variety. Naturally these effects only suit music of an extremist character, but even in less adventurous types of vocal works, the expressive power of consonants should not be ignored.

9. *Vocal Range*

Most contemporary writers require a vocal range which would at one time have been considered impractical—two octaves and a fourth is in frequent demand. This large range, and the equally forbidding requirement of absolute pitch, have made singers of contemporary music as scarce as white sparrows. However, a vocal range of two octaves should not be an unreasonable demand and should suit most expressive purposes.

10. *Design of Vocal Melody*

In vocal melody of a non-traditional kind, the form and design are obviously governed by the poetic text. The best approach is to decide which parts of the text are of 'narrative' type and which are lyrical. The first can then tend towards declamation and the latter towards melismatic expression.

If the text is analysed, points of climax and repose can be decided on and graduated according to importance and intensity. A graph of 'emotive tension values' can then be drawn (as described in the chapter on writing melody) and this, coupled with the subdivision of the vocal part into declamation and melisma, will give the general background design of the melody. Even if this method is only used as a means of roughly sketching in the hills and valleys of the vocal landscape, it can be of considerable value in moulding the work into good proportions and producing effective tension-flow and contrast.

11. Modification of the Text

As music spreads a poem over a much greater time-span than when it is spoken, it is often necessary to abbreviate a text. A poet frequently interpolates secondary thoughts into his main discourse and though these 'asides' are welcome enough when the poem is read, they can be tedious and superfluous in a musical setting.

For instance, in Shakespeare's *Henry IV, Part 2*, the following lines contain secondary phrases which could badly impede the creation of a satisfactory musical design:

> *Why rather, sleep, liest thou in smoky cribs,*
> *Upon uneasy pallets stretching thee*
> *And hush'd with buzzing night-flies to thy slumber,*
> *Than in the perfum'd chambers of the great,*
> *Under the canopies of costly state,*
> *And lull'd with sound of sweetest melody?*

Rather than rush through the whole text in a hasty, declamatory manner, it would be possible to treat only a small portion of the words in more lyrical, expansive fashion. In this way, only two lines are really necessary:

> *Why rather, sleep, liest thou in smoky cribs,*
> *Than in the perfum'd chambers of the great?*

But of course such abbreviation is excessive. The best solution needs much less drastic cutting of the original and only eliminates the two least important lines:

> *Why rather, sleep, liest thou in smoky cribs,*
> *Upon uneasy pallets stretching thee,*
> *Than in the perfum'd chambers of the great,*
> *And lull'd with sound of sweetest melody?*

In this way the main body of the poem remains intact, but it is brought into more manageable proportions.

The converse is sometimes the case. A text may be too short for a musical setting, especially when the words call for a big musical canvas. The only solution here is word repetition—a good old-fashioned recipe, which we seem a bit afraid to use nowadays. But past composers have certainly shown that to paint a big musical picture, it is better to repeat a small number of powerful words, than to plough through any amount of discursive verbosity.

Other forms of repetition are not infrequent. For instance, the first portion of a poem may be repeated at the end of a composition, in order to give more definition to the musical form, or a choir may repeat a setting of words heard previously, while a soloist sings a new section and so on.

Students often seem reluctant to abbreviate a text, or to repeat any part of it, but such treatment is often inevitable if a poem is to suit a musical purpose.

CHORAL MUSIC

In the main, choral music in the serial or twelve-note style has been much less adventurous than music for solo voice. We have already quoted two examples of choral music, from Stravinsky's *Canticum Sacrum* (Ex. 98) and Webern's *Das Augenlicht* (Ex. 95). If both these examples were written out using notes in a diatonic or modal scheme, the result would be very little different from Renaissance music. This is typical of most of the choral music composed up to about 1950. The actual choral *forms* have been archaic, polyphonic and homophonic writing in the Renaissance manner has been quite common, but as the *notes* have been derived from series, the actual sound result has seemed anything but archaic.

The reason for this use of archaic forms has been chiefly one of compromise. Choirs find enough difficulty in pitching the right notes, without having to deal with any other unfamiliar details. It has therefore been found convenient to set the choral parts in familiar traditional forms and with familiar rhythmic outlines. Many old canonic usages have been revived and the re-discovery of the medieval principles of proportional imitation were hailed not long ago as a great innovation. But the truth is that the use of these archaic forms is little more than a subterfuge dictated by the limitations of any but the most specialized body of singers.

In the meantime, one of the greatest innovations in choral music has been the use of the spoken chorus. Dallapiccola and Luigi Nono have used this with considerable effect and recently Sylvano Bussotti extended the idea by using what one might call a 'noise chorus' in one of his compositions. This choir did anything but sing and it is perhaps significant that he preferred to use non-musicians!

However, to return to the purer realms of music, it would seem that the formation of one or two special choirs is now bringing about choral compositions which can abandon archaic forms. The choral works of Luigi Nono, even though only nine in number, already form a solid corpus of choral music in which archaic forms are eliminated. The choral writing tends to be sparse, the vocal parts resembling writing in an instrumental, pointilliste manner. Each part has usually little continuity and as will be seen from the following example, even the separate syllables of words are thrown from one part to another. Much reliance for effect is placed on dynamic contrasts, producing an impression of extreme anguish and

especially later in this same chorus, when the choir is sub-divided into twelve parts, the performance presents extreme difficulties:

Ex. 117

Nono: *Il Canto Sospeso*

Further examples of Nono's choral writing may be found later in Exx. 142 and 145.

12. ORCHESTRATION, TEXTURE, AND TONE COLOUR

ORCHESTRATION

In serial works, instrumental colour and texture have become principal elements of composition and contribute equally with other compositional factors towards the success of the finished composition. In fact, instrumental colour is not infrequently the compositional element of greatest importance. We must therefore discuss orchestration and instrumentation to some extent here, though in this limited space we can deal only with generalities and not with small detail.

Though Schoenberg's occasional orchestral compositions (apart from the two Chamber Symphonies) were scored for the large late-romantic orchestra (quadruple woodwind, four horns, seven or eight brass, and correspondingly large string section) such large forces are not typical of the main run of serial compositions. Schoenberg's orchestration, when such large forces are used, often follows the traditional principle of doubling parts, as may be seen in the following example from his Variations for Orchestra Op. 31 (1927–28):

Ex: 118
The main thematic element of the music is to be found in the quaver movement played for five bars by all four horns. This is taken over by the three trumpets (bar 340) and then passes into the lower registers of the orchestra by the unison doubling of the horns by the first trombone and then the addition of bass clarinet, three bassoons, double bassoon, four trombones, tuba, and double basses. Against this quaver movement there is an ostinato in the lower strings for five bars (in *unison*, for the double bass part is written in real sounds)[1] coupled with chordal passages formed by doubling the upper strings and upper woodwind. However, this doubling of upper strings and woodwind is only real in the last two bars of the example. Previously, the woodwind has sustained the short notes of the strings and *vice versa*. The trumpets sustain a string chord in the first bar, later they play independent staccato chords. In the last four bars, the highest string notes are doubled also by the glockenspiel.

Here Schoenberg has resorted to the doubling of parts in order to achieve sheer volume, using an orchestral technique which is completely traditional in principle. Individuality of orchestral colour has here been completely sacrificed in favour of weight—a procedure which has fallen out of favour and which Schoenberg himself often avoids most carefully. In much of his work he adopts a very different method. There is great individuality of part-writing with constant *contrast* of colour. Doubling is avoided and each melodic or contrapuntal phrase is played by a different instrument in order to obtain ever-changing effects of timbre:

[1]In many modern scores, all transpositions are ignored, and the whole of the score is written in *real sounds* as in these examples from Schoenberg's Op. 31. However, many composers transpose the parts of octave-transposing instruments such as the piccolo, double bass, celesta, glockenspiel, etc.

IX. VARIATION

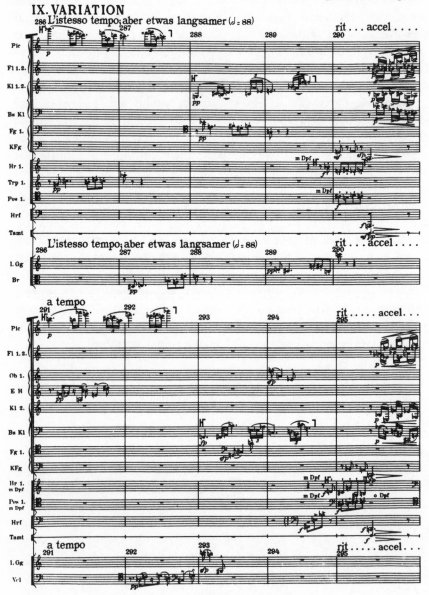

This play of instrumental colour, so typical of much of Schoenberg's work and now widely used by many composers, can be traced as far back as his Five Pieces for Orchestra Op. 16 (1908) in which he already foreshadowed a principle of orchestration which has become a fundamental tool in the serial composer's technical resources. This is the *Klangfarbenmelodie*—the 'melody of sound colours'.

In the third piece of Op. 16 Schoenberg deliberately subjugated every compositional element to this 'melody of sound colours'. He instructs the conductor to make sure that only the differences in tone colour are noticeable and says, 'there are no motivs in this piece which have to be brought to the fore'. The *Klangfarbenmelodie* spreads throughout the piece by gently fluctuating chords, each changing almost imperceptibly in colour through a chain of various instrumental combinations:

Ex. 120   Schoenberg: *5 Pieces for Orchestra*, Op.16

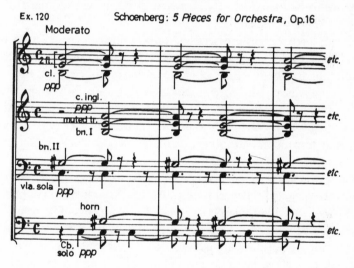

In reality, of course, *Klangfarbenmelodie* is not conventional melody at all, but a colouristic means by which musical interest may be maintained even where melodies do not exist.

The principle of *Klangfarbenmelodie* is naturally more efficiently produced by an orchestra of varied solo instruments than by the massive late-romantic orchestra. This, coupled with the post-1918 anti-romantic movement's aversion to the use of massive forces, has brought about a considerable use of the chamber orchestra of solo instruments.

We therefore find that Webern, the most anti-traditional member of the Viennese School, used a large orchestra only in his Passacaglia Op. 1 (1908). After this, he never used the full orchestra, but only chamber groups comprising various numbers of soloists. Even his Symphony Op. 21 (his most 'conventional' orchestra) is scored for only clarinet, bass clarinet, two horns, harp, and string orchestra.

However, in recent years the use of large orchestral forces has returned. Yet *Klangfarbenmelodie* is still a prime factor. Experience with electronic music has led composers to aspire to much more complex colour effects than a chamber orchestra can produce, and in such works as Stockhausen's *Gruppen* for three orchestras, the virtuoso play of timbres, both for solo instruments and in mass ensembles, is quite fantastic.

However, the modern large orchestra has now acquired a new section of considerable importance. This new section—the percussion—is naturally only an expansion of the old timpani, drums, and cymbals group. But the new percussion section is no longer just a noise-maker. It has risen in importance to be the equal of woodwind, brass, or strings, particularly because of its colour possibilities.

The modern percussion section contains instruments of two different categories—those which produce notes of definite pitch and those of indefinite pitch. The former include the celesta, glockenspiel, tubular bells, xylophone, marimba, vibraphone, cimbalon, mandoline, guitar, piano, harp, tympani, etc. The latter (instruments of indefinite pitch) increase in number almost day by day and include an infinite variety of drums, bongos, tom-toms, cymbals, gongs, tamtams, wood blocks, Chinese blocks, claves, maracas, cabacas, and so on.

The proficiency of percussion players is growing apace, and the best results are obtained when the composer designs his percussion parts so that each player can play a large number of instruments. The result is much more unified than if a large number of players are used for the same instruments. The following example shows what an expert player can do and will reveal the virtuoso possibilities of the percussion section much better than several pages of text could do:[2]

[2]The instruments specified are: triangles, bottles, cow bells, foot cymbals, suspended cymbals, tam-tams, xylophone and vibraphone.

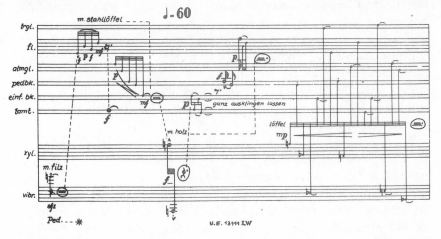

Apart from this growth of the percussion section, the orchestra has
changed little since Strauss, except for the inclusion of the saxophones and
the occasional use of unusual instruments such as the contrabass clarinet,
sarrusophone, flugelhorn, etc.

So much for the forces at our disposal today. We must now briefly consider the general *method* of orchestration in serial music. Here we can
formulate a number of general principles:

1. Instruments are usually used in a *solo* manner, thus achieving maximum individuality of timbre (but mass string writing is common).

2. Doubling of instruments (except in (3) and (4) below) is usually
avoided, as the mixing of instrumental colours tends to obscure individual
qualities of timbre. The old conception of orchestral doubling (e.g. when
upper strings are doubled by the upper woodwind, and the lower strings
by horns and bassoons) is therefore quite abandoned.

3. Instruments are occasionally doubled by one or two of the same
species (e.g. three horns) where the volume of one instrument would be
insufficient, or to achieve a sudden crescendo.

4. A percussion instrument of definite pitch frequently doubles a non-
percussive instrument on a note where a special impact effect may be
required.

5. Octave doublings are usually completely eliminated except for occasional colour effects.

6. The principle of maximum variety of colour, or *Klangfarbenmelodie*,
is used to a considerable extent, and calls for constant changes in tone
colour. However this must be planned both on a large scale (i.e. colour
contrasts between large musical sections) and on a small scale (for variety

of timbre within the smaller parts). This preservation of different colours for different principal sections of the composition must be carefully observed. Otherwise the constant use of *all* the possible orchestral colours will only result in that monotony which extreme variety can cause.

If instruments are to be used in a solo manner and cannot be doubled, the student may well ask how he can use a full orchestra. Part of the answer is that he does not need to. Many serial compositions for orchestra employ its full forces only for very brief spells. But of course this is not a completely satisfactory solution.

The real answer is twofold. Using the principle of *Klangfarbenmelodie*, the changes in instrumentation may be so rapid (see pointillisme mentioned later) that a large number of players may be employed in a short space of time. This is especially the case where various 'horizontal' parts are each expanded into chordal 'blocks' which alternate and intermingle rapidly with each other to produce a kaleidoscopic profusion of colour.

Secondly, and most fundamentally, *an orchestral work must be orchestral in conception*. It must not be a work for chamber orchestra with additions. The use of *Klangfarbenmelodie* in chamber music style is frequently used with full orchestra, yet its effect is altogether too meagre to produce the effect of *mass* which is the orchestra's function. This can only be done by using multiple sounds and rich mixtures of sounds. To this end each group of the orchestra (wind, brass, strings, and percussion) has its own function, or, alternatively, a number of self-contained instrumental groups may be formed from combinations of various instruments. Though contributing to the general musical discourse in varying degrees, each 'group' or sub-group must have an independent part which is seldom duplicated by any other group. The musical discourse is therefore an amalgam of various contemporaneous musical strands, some coming out prominently, others remaining as a discreet background. This means, in general, that the parts for each orchestral section are built up from different types of rhythmic configurations. Some parts may be sustained, others staccato and widely spaced. Some may have rapid movement, others slow. The most important strands of the music will be louder, the subordinate ones softer, and so on. In a great climax, the whole orchestra may be divided into many different parts, to produce a mighty avalanche of sound, but in tranquil sections the texture may thin out considerably to little more than chamber orchestra dimensions.

As an example of orchestration in which various musical strands are amalgamated and in which separate instrumental groups each have their own function, we quote the final bars of the author's *Homage to H. G. Wells:*

Brindle: Homage to H.G. Wells

The musical texture is very complex, designed to produce a turbulent climax and to this end the orchestra is divided into many sections and sub-sections, each playing music of a different character based on specific rhythms used throughout this movement and here combined in their entirety for the first time. As will be seen, the various musical strands (mostly comprising the various rhythms filled out in the form of chords) are allotted to instrumental groups as follows[2]:

Piccolo, flute, and 1st clarinet.
2nd clarinet and two bassoons.
3 horns in unison.
3 trumpets.
3 trombones and tuba.
Bells and piano.
Glockenspiel, vibraphone and upper strings.
Drums and cymbals.
Tam tams.
Timpani.
Lower strings.

It will be noted that the doubling of parts is virtually eliminated. Only in the final chord is there any deliberate doubling, as in the bassoons, tuba, and lower string parts.

Naturally, this is a somewhat extreme example of the division of the orchestral forces into independent sections. There are too many simultaneous events for all the details to be clearly audible and such complexity need only be resorted to in order to create deliberately dense and exciting textures. Normally we would use such orchestration techniques with much more moderation if clarity and intelligibility of discourse are aimed at.

Obviously, in the case of such dense textures combining many diverse orchestral parts, the serial writing will be very complex. In all probability, all twelve notes of the total chromatic will be in almost continuous and simultaneous use. Inevitably, the use of the series becomes virtually pointless and many composers resort to 'free' twelve-note writing, maintaining all twelve notes in constant circulation.

Pointillisme is a term used for a style of serial composition which combines the maximum isolation of sounds with the most extreme use of *Klangfarbenmelodie*. In pointillistic works, the changes in instrumental colour reach a maximum, often accompanied by strong dynamic contrasts. No instrument plays more than one or two notes before the 'melody' is passed over to another instrument of different tone colour:

[2]All sounds in the score are *real sounds* except for the usual octave transpositions (piccolo, double basses and glockenspiel).

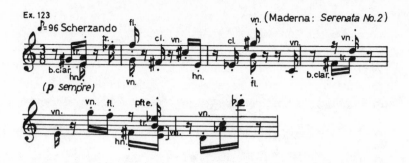

Ex. 123

♩=96 Scherzando   (Maderna: *Serenata No.2*)

(*p sempre*)

As will be seen from the above example, the timbric attractions of *Klangfarbenmelodie* can often be the only element of interest in music which lacks other virtues. *Klang farbenmelodie* has the excellent quality of giving allure to an otherwise barren conception. Nevertheless, this does not detract in any way from the legitimacy of *Klangfarbenmelodie* itself, nor from its great value as a compositional factor. But the student must beware of pursuing its attractions to the exclusion of all other musical values.

As a fine example of the use of *pointillisme* in the large orchestra we quote a typical page from Luigi Nono's *Il Canto Sospeso:*

Ex: 124

$(\flat = ca. 92)$

Nono: Il Canto Sospeso

This page has been chosen from the central climax of the first movement, a movement which sets the tragic, agonized tone of the whole work. *Pointillisme* is one of the chief means of creating the intense atmosphere of suffering, the isolated, stabbing sounds seeming like spasms of pain which torture those who await the Nazi execution squads. Throughout the movement no instrument plays more than two consecutive notes, in fact single notes are more common. Dynamic contrasts are extreme. In a single bar we may find piano alongside fortissimo, indeed sometimes the dynamic contrasts are such that some instruments must remain inaudible. It will be noted that unison doublings are very rare (double basses and trombone in bar 3, or violas and horns 1 and 2 in bar 4) and where they do occur the notes have different time values and dynamics. Octave doublings are completely absent. Though the score has a metrical indication of 4/8, no sense of metre emerges because of the irregular placing of notes. In fact the general effect is deliberately enigmatic, with an intense feeling of disquietude and foreboding of tragedy.

The search for novelties of timbre has brought about a further practice in orchestration, in that changes of instrumental colour are achieved not only by using different instruments, but by varying the tone quality of each individual instrument. This has brought about a profusion of various instrumental effects:

1. *Strings*

bowed
- normal
- at the bridge
- on the fingerboard

pizzicato
- normal
- at the bridge
- rebounding off the fingerboard

harmonics
- natural
- artificial

tremolando
- l.h. tremolando
- bowed tremolando

col legno—bowed with the wood of the bow
col legno battuto—strings beaten with the wood of the bow

glissando
- bowed
- pizzicato

beating the body of the instrument (with the hand or bow)
flautato
trills

controlled vibrato $\begin{cases}\text{slow} \\ \text{medium} \\ \text{fast}\end{cases}$

quarter-tone fluctuations
bowing between the bridge and tailpiece
2. *Brass and Horns*

mutes $\begin{cases}\text{fibre (hard tone)} \\ \text{cup mute (soft tone)}\end{cases}$

fluttertongue
glissando
'stopped' notes (horns)
3. *Woodwind*
mutes (bassoon, saxophone, etc.)
fluttertongue
harmonics (single)
harmonics (multiple)
tone variations
controlled vibrato (various speeds)
quarter-tone fluctuations
glissandi
tremolos
'breathed' sounds
'key noise' sounds
4. *Percussion*
  Effects are too numerous to list in detail, but an important factor to bear in mind is that most percussion instruments have a wide variety of sounds according to the type of beater or drum-stick employed. Beaters and sticks may be soft (felt-covered or soft rubber) or hard (hard rubber, plastic, ebonite, or wood). Drums, tympani, and cymbals may be struck with side drum sticks, soft or hard tympani sticks, wire brushes, vibraphone beaters, etc.

  This large variety of possible colour effects in each single instrument is now considerably exploited. Unfortunately some composers make a fetish of these devices, and the bewildered performer must often wonder if all the effort is really worthwhile:

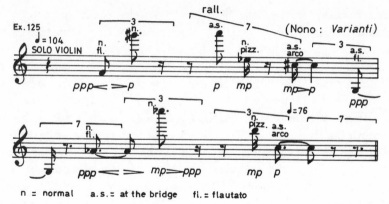

Ex: 125

In these *Varianti* of Luigi Nono, the solo violinist has not only a different dynamic indication for every note, but each note in the whole piece has its individual colour indication. One cannot help but feel that this desperate research for effect is either a purely mechanical routine, or a desire to show off the composer's *bravura* in instrumentation. One thing is certain, in dealing with individual instrumental effects we must be careful that we do not forget the equation:

$$\text{extreme variety} = \text{extreme monotony.}$$

A FEW RECOMMENDATIONS

Beware of colouristic change for its 'paper' value.

Beware of mechanical instrumentation routines.

Don't use *all* the orchestral colours *all* the time.

Preserve colour contrast between various sections of a work.

Distinguish between writing for chamber orchestra and for full orchestra.

Get to know every instrument.

Don't write a piece and orchestrate it afterwards.

Above all, think in orchestral terms. Create each instrumental colour, each phrasing, each nuance, as you create each individual sound.

TEXTURE

Texture is a vital element in contemporary music, just as it is modern painting and sculpture. Indeed in some paintings form and colour are so subordinated to surface texture that the texture *is* the painting. Of course, these are extreme cases. Nevertheless a canvas which is merely glazed and a stone which is polished, now have less aesthetic appeal (other things being equal!) than others with more adventurous surfaces.

Similarly, in music texture can be a predominant factor in the com-, poser's vision It is often the first discernible element in his process of conception. Yet there is no adequate definition of texture in music dictionaries, and *Grove* ignores its existence completely.

Texture, in one sense, can be defined as structure, or the 'arrangement of constituent parts'. But, though we may speak of a 'contrapuntal texture', the exact species or kind of counterpoint cannot be described by such terminology. We are referring to the general kind of *sound*, rather than to the precise kind of *construction*. The alternative definition of texture as 'grain, web, surface, or nap' is nearer the mark. It defines the outside 'feel' of the music, rather than the inner structure. The adjectives usually used with musical 'texture' confirm this definition—'rough, smooth, thick, thin, warm, cold, heavy, rich, meagre, gossamer, silky, velvet, jagged'— all these describe exterior sensations.

Our awareness of exterior texture is immediate, whereas our recognition of inner structure is a slower process. It is just like the feel of a piece of cloth, which can tell us more, in a fraction of a second, than any amount of detailed analysis of its composition.

This, then, is the texture which is so important in music—its exterior sensation. But even now our definition is not couched in precise musical terms. This is because the musical factors which contribute to texture are elusive and not easily defined, nor are they constant in every situation. Musical texture is a subtle amalgam of various elements—instrumental colour, density, pitch, movement, rhythmic configuration, etc. All these factors are usually present, though their relative importance will vary in every situation.

The precise musical components of textures have never been catalogued, nor is it possible to do so here. What is important is that the student should become *aware* of texture, so that his work may be enriched and given more definition. He should cultivate a subtle variation in textures rather than constancy. An orchestral movement by Bach was usually based on a single texture throughout, or on quite limited texture changes or contrasts. This was because musical interest was concentrated in the thematic, harmonic and contrapuntal elements. Today the story is quite different, and without subtle mutations of texture, music can lack one of its most vital dimensions. The student should, therefore, practise texture contrast—the contrast of density with sparseness, icy coldness with passionate warmth, complexity with simplicity, brittle, splintering sounds with mellowness, and so on. Textures can then be superimposed or gradually transformed. In this way, he will expand his technique, and have more resources at his disposal.

The only factor in sound production which governs the colour or 'timbre' of a sound is the presence or absence of overtones and their relative strength or weakness in relation to the fundamental tone. Overtones give a sound its characteristic quality. So all instrumental sounds are combination sounds, consisting of a predominant tone and various overtones, harmonics or 'upper partials'. They can vary from the simple mellow flute sound (a predominant tone with very few quiet harmonics) to the strident muted trumpet (with strong upper partials) or to the cymbal clash, with its harsh jangle of dissonant tones and overtones. Sounds with few overtones are smooth, pure, euphonious, and often subdued in character. Those with many and complex overtones may be harsh, penetrating, pungent, virile, and even jarringly discordant.

Each orchestral instrument also has a variety of timbres in its various registers, and/or at different volumes. For instance, the low register of the flute, when blown softly, can be mellow (lacking overtones), or when blown louder can be almost harsh (rich in overtones). The upper notes can be dull harmonic sounds, or piercingly brilliant. Similarly the chalumeau register of the clarinet can be rich and pungent, or softly subdued, and so on.

It is important to realize which instrumental sounds have little overtone content (and therefore tend towards mellowness and smoothness), which are richer (giving virile sounds), and which have strong and complex overtone contents (tending towards harshness).

Once this information is acquired, the process of orchestration can be carried out on sure ground, with more certainty of success. For every orchestral colour and texture can be made up of just those component sounds which contribute most efficiently towards the desired effect (provided balance is observed).

Orchestration will also become much more subtle, for we can learn to merge timbres, modify them, and transform them ingeniously. Whereas previously we would tend to use each family of instruments as 'blocks' of tone colour, we can now use more skilful combinations of instruments to produce more refined effects. For instance, if we require a quiet but virile-sounding chord we could choose to use quiet muted brass—a 'safe' solution. But later we could learn to use more subtle means to produce the same effect, adding an intangible quality which makes the original 'all brass' sound seem comparatively crude. We may choose to use such a combination as:

(mp) oboe (middle register)
(p) trumpet with fibre mute (middle register)
(mf) flute (low register, but rich in overtones)
(mp) clarinet (chalumeau register)
(mp) viola (open C string, at the bridge)
(pp) vibraphone tremolo (hard hammers, motor off)
(p) pianoforte (upper register)
(pp) cymbal roll (wire brushes)

Here is a mixture of instrumental sounds, some of them 'thin' and virile, others less so, but the more 'mellow' instruments (flute, clarinet and viola) play in registers and at volumes which will produce virile sounds, rich in overtones, which will merge well with the oboe and trumpet. The dynamic signs for each instrument are such that balance is maintained and also the right quality of tone is produced. The piano gives an initial hard attack, while the vibraphone tremolo and cymbal roll produce a brittle shimmer which clothes and unifies the other sounds into one luminous whole.

However, this does not mean that instruments should always be mixed, and that the use of separate family groups of instruments should always be avoided. Indeed excessive and continuous mixing of tone colours is to be guarded against. For there is the danger that excessive mixing produces only a mono-colour effect, just as a rapid succession of all the colours of the spectrum produces white light.

The ideal orchestration is where the simple pure colour of family groups is maintained amid a more complex situation of change, where timbres are merged, transformed, modified, and mixed as occasion demands.

Like the painter, the orchestrator has a palette of primary colours. They are merely crude when used alone, but when mixed they give subtle intermediary shades. But once the intermediary shades are formed, primary colours can be re-introduced with the most powerful effect of all

13. STYLISTIC FACTORS

Stylistic Originality Versus Stylistic Purity. Available Styles.

STYLISTIC ORIGINALITY VERSUS STYLISTIC PURITY

The sheer mechanics of serialism are easy enough to learn, but to turn the system into well-sculptured music is quite another matter. For composition means (amongst other things) the communication of emotions and ideas through a language which is compatible with the compositional technique employed—in other words, thoughts must be expressed through a musical *style* which goes hand in glove with the *method* used. With serialism, students often fail to write interesting, well-defined compositions because their knowledge of the available styles is inadequate, or because they choose a style, which, though 'correct', does not suit their own individual expressive needs.

Students should therefore not only acquire a good grounding in serial technique, they should also be well acquainted with all the musical styles used in serialism since the early twenties. Their compositional work should also be allied to studies of recent musical history and aesthetics—for to use any idiom with conviction, it is essential not only to know how and why it was created, but to be in accord also with its aesthetic premises.

So many student compositions are also stylistically nondescript because young musicians feel compelled to be stylistically 'original'. But is it so necessary to be original in style? The truth is that we make too much of a fetish of stylistic originality. Not only is it quite impossible for thousands of composers to write in thousands of different styles, but if they did, the consequences would be undesirable. We would be lost in an incomprehensible labyrinth of fashions, artistic trends would lose direction, and in all probability musical progress would disintegrate.

Certainly we have seen tremendous changes of fashion in music since 1945, but there is now every sign that for the time being the rate of change is slowing down. But even so, it is certain that what to us seem great stylistic differences, may in the long run be of little permanent significance. For in two hundred years' time people will probably see very little difference between Berg and Dallapiccola, Webern and Boulez, or even between Stravinsky and Schoenberg.

Everything is of relative importance and we must see things in their historical perspective. If we can do this, we may decide that stylistic purity (in existing idioms) is much more important than stylistic individuality. After all, Bach and Mozart were only too happy to use the well-tried language of their predecessors. They have proved that immortality is achieved not by creating new fashions, but by moving the hearts of men through a language which is common property and familiar to all.

This question of stylistic familiarity is just as important today. When our music is already largely incomprehensible even to the most ardent amateurs, it is important to maintain stylistic consistency in order that idioms may become familiar and the musical content easily assimilated.

It therefore seems that though stylistic exploration is certainly not to be ignored, it is only for the few. For the vast majority, stylistic purity in existing idioms should be aimed at and originality demonstrated in *what* is expressed rather than *how* it is said.

Such concepts would probably be energetically disputed by the more extreme elements of the *avant-garde* and their camp followers. But their aggressive policy of change and revolution merely demonstrates either that change is pursued for its own sake, or that the products of their school have such impermanence that ceaseless change has become a policy of necessity.

In stylistic matters we should have no inhibitions, nor should we allow ourselves to be coerced into stylistic paths which do not suit our own fantasy. Our prime considerations must be communicability and faithfulness to our own ideals and instincts.

AVAILABLE STYLES

It is certainly possible to use serial or free twelve-note compositional techniques with virtually any musical style. We have already seen these techniques allied to Renaissance and Baroque contrapuntal idioms, classical styles, and the more abstract patterns of Webern and the post-Webernian *avant-garde*. Serial techniques can even be used in music of a lighter vein—the lilting *Ländler* and waltz motifs and Carinthian folk-tune in Berg's Violin Concerto are good examples—and there is every evidence that serialism is becoming a stimulating factor in the jazz field.

Serialism is very adaptable. It could be used to write anything from a national anthem to a calypso. But we must have aesthetic discrimination. In all cases, the suitability or otherwise of the serial method to the stylistic medium is of paramount importance. For the truth is that serialism can in many cases only *distort* those musical styles which were the vehicles of creative thought in tonal spheres. Much classical music of the homophonic or melody-and-accompaniment type depends so much for its effect on tranquil, seemingly inevitable harmonic movement, that to ally it with the restless, unquiet harmonies of serialism is to produce only a nightmare caricature which is aesthetically distasteful. A great deal of classical music is so intimately allied with the cheerful air of the major triad or to the sweet pathos of the minor chord that to wed such styles to the complex chromatic resultants of serialism is incongruous. It would be an ingenious composer indeed who could make a serialist madrigal or Mozartian aria sound anything but the work of a neurotic personality.

Great skill is therefore needed to wed serialism successfully with a predominantly harmonic style. But with contrapuntal forms, the story is different. Ever since the chromatic fantasias of the Renaissance, polyphony has proved an excellent medium for highly chromatic writing. It is therefore quite logical that contrapuntal styles have become natural instruments of serialism. However, exclusively contrapuntal writing is no complete solution to the stylistic problem. In excessive quantities, polyphony can become very tedious. Inevitably we all have to face the necessity, sooner or later, of finding a style in which all musical elements (including melody, harmony, and counterpoint) can co-exist in a satisfactory relationship, that the resulting style should form a happy union with the compositional technique used (serial or otherwise) and that the total result is a completely adequate and suitable form of self-expression.

In order to illustrate the wide selection of styles which are available in serial music, a dozen examples are now quoted. Though these by no means represent all stylistic possibilities, they show the main types and reveal the enormous contrasts of style which have existed over only three decades.

1. *Serialization of Baroque homophonic (or polyphonic) styles*

Ex. 126

Berg : *Violin Concerto*

The violin melody is that of Ahle's chorale 'Es ist genug' (1662). Though the wide-spanning arpeggios in bars 1 and 6 are not typical of Baroque writing, the remaining parts are not far removed from Baroque figuration. The music is far from atonal, indeed it tends rather towards traditional chromatic harmony. In the above example tonal relationships are sometimes quite clear (e.g. the dominant-tonic cadence in A minor to be found in bar 4), at others they are obscured (as in the last bar) but Berg's aim has obviously been that of preserving euphony throughout.

2. Serialization of Renaissance contrapuntal techniques

This is a double canon, the outer parts forming one canon, the inner parts the other. The triplet movement would be unusual in Renaissance music, otherwise the rhythmic designs and overall form are true to type. The inner parts use transposed 'I' forms of the series found in the outer parts. In general, the harmony formed is fairly consonant, even tonal but this is disrupted by harsh non-tonal note groups at certain points.

3. Light Music

Ex.128 Scherzando
(immer vier oder zweitaktig, wie ein Walzer)

Berg : *Violin Concerto*

This is typical of various sections in the Scherzo of Berg's Violin Concerto. Though the accompaniment here is unambiguously in F major, the chromatic intricacy of the upper parts results in music of a fairly complex harmonic character. A much more simple result could be obtained by clarifying the upper parts, reducing the restlessness of the harmony by note repetitions, etc.

4. *Melody and simple chordal accompaniment (classical style)*

Ex.129

Mario Peragallo: *Violin Concerto*

p serenamente espressivo

This passage is remarkably simple, yet very effective. The violin part would seem to be entirely in a transposed mixolydian mode, while the accompaniment uses only four basic chords (with two slight alterations). The rhythmic figurations are completely classic throughout. The first four bars of the violin part repeat rhythm 'A', bars 6 and 7 use rhythm 'B'. The last bar is a variant of rhythm 'A'. Only the fifth bar departs from this scheme of classic regularity.

This pattern of melody and chordal accompaniment is also very frequently used in styles which avoid any classical associations by non-repetition of rhythms, irregular patternings, etc.

5. *Melody and freely contrapuntal accompaniment (non-classical)*

Ex: 130

The melody in the first violin is accompanied by brief, incisive counterpoints in strong contrast with the sustained quality of the melody. Rhythms and metres are irregular and avoid any classical associations.

6. *Classical chamber music and symphonic style*

Ex.131   Schoenberg: *3rd String Quartet*

Though the writing is apparently quite complex, the music is formed by the repetition of a small number of thematic cells not far removed in style from that of Beethoven's later period. In its rhythmic configuration the whole of this quartet adheres closely to the Beethoven manner.

7. *Homophonic chordal style*

Ex.132

Dallapiccola : - *Il Prigioniero*

This example quotes two motifs of Dallapiccola's opera, the 'fratello' motif in the upper string part, and the echoing 'Roelandt' theme in the muted trumpet and oboe. The homophonic string writing in seven and eight parts comprises the 'fratello' motif above and parallel streams of minor chords (with sevenths) below. The remaining inner parts complete serial functions, roughly following the 'fratello' design. The general plan is therefore one of two streams of parallel chords in upper and lower string parts, moving in contrary motion. Of course, exclusively homophonic writing has only a limited use, but its simplicity and directness can be extremely effective, especially as a contrast to more complex contrapuntal sections.

8. *Impressionist style*

Ex.133

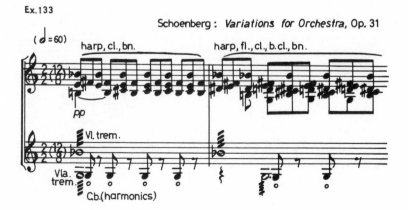

Schoenberg : *Variations for Orchestra*, Op. 31

Though the impressionist style is far removed aesthetically from the general tenets of serial composers, nevertheless it sometimes reveals itself in passages which express a tentative, delicate mood. The vagueness of twelve-note harmony suits this style admirably, especially if more delicate harmonies are allowed to predominate, as in the above example.

9. Strict counterpoint in the Webern manner

This double canon comprises a canon between the outer parts and another canon between the inner parts. The whole is a mirror structure. Phrases are brief and disjointed, especially through the alternation of arco and pizzicato. The resulting effect is enigmatic and the highly organized nature of the music is not easily perceived by purely auditory means.

10. *Free counterpoint in the post-Webern manner.*

Here there is no common thematic material and no contrapuntal relationship between the parts. Though the music is rhythmically very complex, this serves only to disperse the feeling of metre, so that the result suggests improvisation rather than music composed through a highly organized system (this quartet was composed with the structures of integral serialism, to be discussed in Chapter 15).

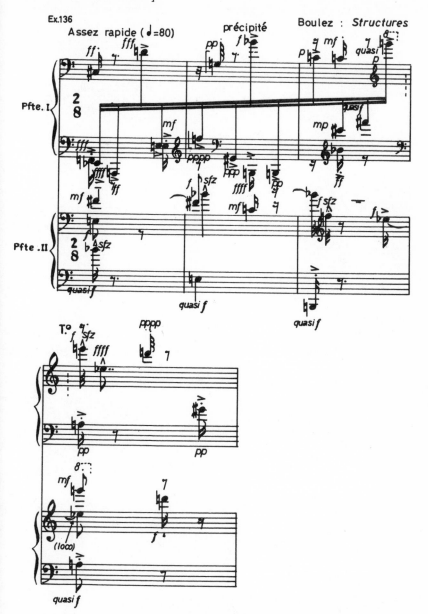

Ex.136   précipité   Boulez : *Structures*

Though there are many varied styles within the *avant-garde* movement, the above example has been chosen as being typical of the general pattern of these compositions. As will be seen, there is even less continuity in the 'voice' parts that in the Maderna example quoted above and all elements

151

of traditional composition are virtually eliminated. These *Structures* were composed by various highly organized methods which will be discussed in a chapter dedicated to *avant-garde* compositions.

12. Jazz

Ex.137   Slow   Brindle: *Chrome Ground*

The main features of jazz—metrical energy, melodic simplicity, and harmonic clarity—are not easily compatible with serial construction. In the above example, metrical energy is prominent, but depends, in the last analysis, on the rhythmic 'ride' produced by the percussion section. Both the vibraphone melody and string bass accompaniment are given coherence by repetition, while the characteristic syncopated 'off beat' rhythms of jazz have not been abandoned. The harmonic problem has been largely avoided by adopting a contrapuntal technique. The result is therefore a compromise. Those elements of jazz have been retained which can be used with serialism, while those aspects of serialism are used which most easily suit the needs of jazz.

These dozen examples of various styles represent only a fraction of what is really necessary to illustrate this subject adequately. Indeed, the various serial and twelve-note styles could well be subject matter for an entire book. In quoting so few examples, the intention is not to present a complete picture, but to show the main stylistic prototypes. They are intended as a point of departure, from which the student should himself investigate the endless variety of possibilities.

14. PERMUTATIONS AND OTHER VARIANTS OF A SERIES

Permutations. Hauer's 'Tropes'. Segmentation

PERMUTATIONS

The derived forms of the series given in Chapter 4 ('I', 'R', and 'RI' versions) are not the only possible variants of a twelve-note series. By varying the order of the series, preferably (but not necessarily) by some logical process, many other variants may be obtained. This method is called permutation, and though it has been little used by composers until recent times, there is evidence of its application even in the Roman era.

Of course, permutation is not only applicable to a series of notes. It can be used to vary the order of any series of objects, ideas, facts, or symbols. But as the basic factor in any series is *number*—the number of its component parts—it is to the permutations of number that we will give our immediate attention.

The principles of permutation of numbers can then later be applied to the permutation of the notes of a twelve-note series, to the six notes in each hexachord (see later in this chapter), to a number of duration values, or dynamic values (see 'Integral Serialism', Chapter 15), or to a number of electronic sound effects, in fact, to many other aspects of composition as well as the ordering of a twelve-note series.

Every series has a fixed number of permutations. For example, for the series 1 2, the only possible variant is 2 1. For the series 1 2 3 there are five variants:

$$
\begin{array}{ccc}
1 & 3 & 2 \\
2 & 1 & 3 \\
2 & 3 & 1 \\
3 & 1 & 2 \\
3 & 2 & 1 \\
\end{array}
$$

The formula $(1 \times 2 \times 3)$ gives the total number of possible forms of a three number series. So the total number of forms of a twelve-note series $= 1 \times 2 \times 3 \times 4 \times 5 \times 6 \times 7 \times 8 \times 9 \times 10 \times 11 \times 12 = 479{,}001{,}600$

Naturally we do not wish to investigate almost 500 million permutations. Nor is it necessary. But as we probably prefer to re-order a series by some logical process,[1] rather than by jumbling up the numbers in any slipshod manner, we will consider a few elementary forms of permutation.

A very straightforward form of permutation is the selection of every other number according to the following design:

the result being: 1 3 5 7 9 11/2 4 6 8 10 12—which, of course, gives odd numbers in order first, then even numbers. For want of a better terminology, we will call this an 'every second' (number) permutation.

Now if we take this first variant and repeat the process, writing down 'every second' number, yet another variant is formed. And so on until nine variants are formed:

(a)	1	3	5	7	9	11	2	4	6	8	10	12
(b)	1	5	9	2	6	10	3	7	11	4	8	12
(c)	1	9	6	3	11	8	5	2	10	7	4	12
(d)	1	6	11	5	10	4	9	3	8	2	7	12
(e)	1	11	10	9	8	7	6	5	4	3	2	12
(f)	1	10	8	6	4	2	11	9	7	5	3	12
(g)	1	8	4	11	7	3	10	6	2	9	5	12
(h)	1	4	7	10	2	5	8	11	3	6	9	12
(i)	1	7	2	8	3	9	4	10	5	11	6	12
	1	2	3	4	5	6	etc.					

If the process is repeated after the ninth variant 'i', we return to the original serial order—1 to 12. The 'every second' process is therefore finite, its possibilities are limited.

---

[1]It may well be asked why we should prefer to re-order a series by some logical process rather than quite arbitrarily. The main reason is surely that the human mind prefers to work methodically, to produce order out of chaos and at the same time create relationships between disparate things. As far back as we can go in the history of art there is evidence of this human instinct to create order, to systematize, to create a unity even while preserving diversity. As for the permutation of a series of notes, it is worth noting that one of the first known examples of this procedure (to be found in an anonymous Roman music manual of the third century A.D.) reveals a methodical re-ordering of a four-note series, and not an arbitrary re-ordering. The four notes A B C and D are permuted as follows:

A B C D
A C B D
A D B C
A B D C
A C D B
A D C B

We can now try a similar process using 'every third' (number) according to the following design:

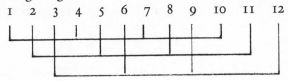

The result is: 1 4 7 10 2 5 8 11 3 6 9 12. But unfortunately we find this is the same as 'h' in 'every second'.

The three other possible variants of the 'every third' permutation are the same as 'f', 'd' and 'b' of the 'every second' method.

Similarly we find that 'every fourth' produces only four variants, the same as 'a', 'b', 'f' and 'h'.

'Every fifth' will not work in this kind of design.

'Every sixth' will work, but only one variant is possible and that the same as 'i' of 'every second'.

This design will not work at 'every seventh' or more.

To sum up this form of permutation—it is finite, and all possible variants are already contained in the nine variants of the 'every second' permutation. Another limitation is that the first and last numbers never change.

Let us try another method. Here the series is laid out in a continuously recurring stream:

1 2 3 4 5 6 7 8 9 10 11 12 1 2 3 4 5 6 7 8 9 10 11 12 1 2 3 4 5 6 7 8 9 etc.
1   6   11   4   9   2   7

If every fifth number is chosen, as above, we obtain the following:

(j) 1 6 11 4 9 2 7 12 5 10 3 8

But this method of permutation is already exhausted, for every fifth number of 'j' brings us back to the original order again. Similarly it will be found that by this system of permutation, only one variant is possible with 'every seventh' number and 'every eleventh' number. This scheme does not work with any other numbers.

However, we now have the possibility of obtaining many more permutations. Using the nine 'every second' variants of the first system on the three new variants of the second, twenty-seven new series are obtained. These new series can then be again permuted and cross permuted by the means at our disposal, to give a new crop of 324 series and so on.

But we have already gone far enough. The composer who needs to go farther is either on a fantastic quest, or in desperate straits indeed.

To restore an air of normality to this discussion, we must observe that as far as the twelve-note series is concerned:

1. not all variants are useful, in fact many of them usually have to be discarded on purely musical grounds.

2. Even with the most elementary permutations, the identity of the original series is hidden. The use of permutations (even to a small extent) means that any unity the original series gives to a composition is thereby dispersed.

However, permutations have not infrequently been used by composers to discover alternative thematic material. Even Berg, whose melodic gifts are quite out of the ordinary, preferred to derive some of the main themes of his opera *Lulu* by permutations of the original series. *But we must stress that thematic material obtained by permutation bears no audible relation to the original series.* Variants produced by permutation are not at all comparable to the integral presentation of a musical shape that is preserved intact in the four serial orders (the 'O', 'I', 'R', and 'RI' forms) and their transpositions. Once permutation begins the original series is abandoned, together with any audible unity it may give to the music. But sometimes the thematic variety obtained by permutation is regarded as an asset. Indeed, some composers deliberately ignore the unifying force of the twelve-note series and the note-order of their music is then determined by a chain of permutations, in which no variant is ever used twice.

Similarly, in 'Integral Serialism' (see Chapter 15 on this subject) the rhythms, duration values, dynamics, and even instrumentation may be derived by permutation.

HAUER'S TROPES

Another important way of ordering the twelve notes of the total-chromatic are the 'tropes' of Josef Matthias Hauer, which, though similar to Schoenberg's series in some respects, are quite different in others. In his publication *Vom Wesen der Musikalischen* (Vienna, 1920), Hauer writes of atonal melody: 'Its law, its *nomos* consists of a perpetual repetition of all twelve notes of the tempered scale'. But instead of observing this principle with its full implications of free, unordered repetition both Hauer and Schoenberg established restrictions on the principle in the name of order, method, unity, and so on. The real truth is possibly that both of them felt at a loss when confronted with the task of dealing with an unordered recurrence of the twelve notes and therefore both of them sought some ordering principle, some way of *facilitating* the perpetual problem of choice (of note orders) with which they were confronted. Schoenberg chose to establish a fixed note order (the series). He put a strait-jacket on the composer's freedom of choice. Hauer instead chose to preserve a reasonable possibility of selection.

Hauer's 'tropes' still include all twelve chromatic notes, but are divided into two six-note segments, or 'hexachords'. No note is repeated in each segment and no note is common to both segments. But the partitioning of the twelve notes into two halves is the only restricting factor. The notes in each hexachord are not set out in any rigid order and the composer has therefore free choice in the ordering of each group of six notes. His only obligation, naturally, is to use each hexachord alternately in order to maintain the 'perpetual repetition of all twelve notes of the tempered scale'.

This system would seem to have many advantages, though it may lack the 'unifying force' of Schoenberg's series. Freedom of choice, at least within each hexachord, means that the composer is less restricted in what he writes both horizontally and vertically. His melody and harmony are therefore liberated from Schoenberg's strict note-orderings and are liable to benefit considerably. 'Free fantasy' and 'inspiration' are set at large within a six-note dimension, which being almost as large as the diatonic scale seven-note dimension, is a fairly generous area.

In reality, many composers who use Schoenberg's twelve-note series often tend to break it up into two hexachords and use the contents of each segment freely. The Schoenberg and Hauer systems can therefore be used in alternation. Even in brief passages, they can exist side by side, and thus unified can give the consistency of the one method and the freedom of the other. The resultant 'method' has much to be recommended if the composer's aspiration is to write music which has the ideal qualities of both constructional logic and free fantasy.

In practice the 'trope' is usually written out so that in each hexachord the notes are arranged in scalic patterns as compositional 'material', without significance in the note ordering. For instance, the series of Webern's Op. 23 (Ex. 27) when written out in trope form would be as follows:

Ex. 138   (Webern's Op.23 series in 'trope' form.)

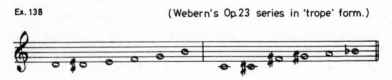

The contents of each hexachord can then be re-ordered at will. In fact, each hexachord can be arranged in 720 different ways. But as many of these variants would contain those formations (e.g. triads, adjacent fourths, whole-tone groups) which compromise the atonal equilibrium and therefore may be considered invalid, the actual number of suitable variants of any given hexachord may be considerably less.

Transpositions of each trope are possible, as with the twelve-note series, but frequently it will be found that the transposition of certain hexachords merely reproduces the same succession of notes (as with the whole-tone scale, where only one transposition is possible).

Tropes are never used in inverted form as inversion would usually (but not always) produce different contents in each hexachord.

Hauer has affirmed that only forty-four tropes are sufficient for the derivation of all possible twelve-note melodies, which, of course, should be the same in number as the 479 million-odd possible twelve-note series.

Obviously, it would seem that given any 'trope', the easiest way of ordering the contents of each hexachord is by some permutational method. A small number of permutations which give satisfactory note-orders, with their relative transpositions, should be sufficient for most compositions. Alternatively, the composer can proceed always by free choice, or combine both methods.

SEGMENTATION

A further extension of Hauer's 'trope' system, is the division of a twelve-note series into various equal segments, each containing either two, three, or four notes. (No one seems to consider the use of unequal segments (e.g. 2+3+2+3+2), though there can be no reasonable objection.) The contents of each segment can then be freely ordered. Also the order of the segments themselves can be varied. Especially if the segments are small (only two or three notes) the contents of some segments will be the same in one or more transposed forms of the series. Such a segment then becomes a 'pivot' between these transposed forms of the series, and as other segment contents will then be in different combinations than in the original, this enables a very varied patterning of note-combinations to be used.

Before closing this chapter, we must try to put into true perspective the whole question of permutation, segmentation, and other variants of the series.

Such usage is probably pursued for one of two reasons:

(1) The composer may genuinely feel the strict order of a series to be a serious limitation on his invention. It may be a constant fetter on his imagination. He therefore seeks some logical process which will give him a more ample amount of basic material and thereby offer him greater freedom of choice. In reality he is fighting for liberation.

(2) On the other hand the composer may regard excessive freedom as anarchy, leading to chaos. In an extreme case his subconscious may fear freedom so intensely that he makes a fetish of 'systems' and imprisons his fantasy within a web of constructional mumbo-jumbo. His work is probably quite ingenious and its structural logic irrefutable. But if it breathes

the breath of life it is a coincidence, if it rises to a moment of ecstasy, it is a miracle.

As for Hauer's 'tropes', the free ordering of the notes in each hexachord is a liberalizing process, but in reality it is only a half measure. Complete liberalization is only achieved when all twelve notes of the total chromatic are freely ordered and controlled. But to control twelve notes (with almost four hundred and eighty million possibilities) is a very different matter from dealing with only six (with only seven hundred and twenty variations). So if our personal expression calls for greater liberty in the use of the total chromatic, Hauer's hexachords can temporarily ease the problem of control, until that day when we can deal with the whole of chromatic space dexterously and with complete mastery.

15. THE AVANT GARDE, INTEGRAL SERIALISM, AND IMPROVISATION

The Avant-Garde. *Integral Serialism. Proportionalisms. Numerical Proportionalisms. Rhythmic Cell Constructions. Rhythmic Construction Through the Series. Improvisation.*

THE AVANT-GARDE

There have always been 'revolutionary' composers who have led music into new paths, and in their day were just as keen on radical reforms as any composer today. The only difference is that they built on tradition, whereas today's *avant-garde* determined on forming a new musical language which aimed at clearing the decks of all convention. Around the mid-century a period of extreme experimentalism began, in which even Schoenberg's compositional techniques were discarded as being too traditional and the aim was to begin anew with a fundamental revision of every element in the musical language.

The reasons for this drastic elimination of the past are many, some purely artistic, others due to political, social, and ideological issues which are beyond the scope of an exclusively technical book. What is important is that already a new musical language has been formed which is concrete and well-defined, and already we can see that it is a link in the chain of evolutions which form tradition itself. In fact, many aspects of early *avant-garde* work can already be seen as foundation stones on which we are now building an increasingly perfected musical language. It will be our object here to examine techniques which have created these building stones and to comment on other present-day compositional usages.

INTEGRAL SERIALISM

The *avant-garde* composer's 'fundamental revision of every element of the musical language' can now be seen to have been only partial and directed more in one direction than in others. As to the basic elements of music—melody, harmony, counterpoint, and form—Schoenberg had already made considerable amendments. With Webern, these factors and others such as rhythmic design, dynamics, orchestration, and tone colour were subjected to even more far-reaching changes.

But Schoenberg left one very important compositional factor largely unrevised—rhythmic configuration—and though Webern made considerable changes in this direction, particularly in the rhythmic organization of such works as his Variations for Orchestra Op. 30, it was in this aspect of music that most possibility of development lay after his death. As we have already noted in our chapter on melody, it is precisely by its rhythmic configuration that the character of music is mainly determined. It is useless adopting serialism with its melodic, harmonic, and formal implications if the rhythmic patterns remain traditional. For repetitive rhythms and their resulting classical continuity of discourse throw the music back into the past.

The main work of the *avant-garde* has been the development of new rhythmic figurations and in the relationship of rhythm to metre. As an inevitable consequence new formal principles have also been devised. All other changes have been of a secondary nature in comparison with these outstanding achievements.

As, in the post-war period, a composer's big problem in dealing with rhythms was the difficulty of erasing from his mind the influence of our musical heritage, he resorted to computational systems by which new rhythmic designs could be created, rhythms which (being born of abstract systems) would be completely unconventional and thereby create music of a new ethos. Soon this principle of computational composition was used not only to determine the music's rhythmic designs, but for all compositional factors (note order, dynamics, instrumentation, silences, etc.) and so the principle of 'total organization' or 'integral serialism' was born.

Though methods of integral serialism are now being abandoned (for they have already served their purpose), their use is an excellent discipline and a good means of exploring new rhythmic possibilities. We will therefore examine a few simple methods of computational composition, which the student can later develop into more complex systems of his own.

PROPORTIONALISMS

One of the most useful means of organizing rhythmic structures is through the use of various forms of basic proportions. The proportions can be either by numbers, or by pre-established rhythmic cells. Both methods are not without precedent in the history of music, in fact proportions by number were used in medieval times.

1. Numerical Proportionalisms

The most elementary way of using proportions by number can be seen in Dallapiccola's *Canti di Liberazione*, where the basic proportion 2 1 1 is used in the first chorus. These proportions form the rhythm ♩ ♪ ♪ and its diminished variants ♪. ♫♩. and ♩ ♫♩ . These rhythms are also used in their retrograde forms ♫♩ , ♫♩. and ♪♪♪ . The composer uses the various forms of the basic proportion quite freely, according to no set plan, and silences are organized according to expressive necessity. This structure, though simple, is made to produce music of a highly poetic nature:

Ex. 139

Dallapiccola : *Canto di Liberazione*

More complex ways of using numerical proportions are to be found in Luigi Nono's *Il Canto Sospeso*.[1] As two completely different ways of using the same proportions can be found in the second movement, for eight-part chorus, we will examine this in some detail.

The movement is built of two structures, the first thirty-four bars long, the second sixteen bars, both parts being based on the series of numerical proportions 1 2 3 5 8 13, but developing it in different ways.

In the first structure the numerical series and its retrograde form (1 2 3 5 8 13/13 8 5 3 2 1) is applied to four basic duration values:

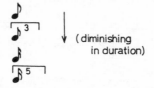

The structure begins with a four-note chord in which the first four numbers of the numerical series (1 2 3 5) are applied to the four duration values in order of diminishing duration. The result is therefore:

[1]A more extended analysis of Nono's *Il Canto Sospeso* was published by the author in *Musical Quarterly* (New York), April, 1962. Some portions have been extracted from this article and are here printed by permission of G. Schirmer, Inc., New York.

the shortest of these notes (♪) is then followed by ₈ₓ ♪ , the next shortest ⌐3⌐♩ by ₁₃ₓ ⌐3⌐♪ , and so on. Whenever a note ends it is followed by another formed by multiplying the same basic duration value by the next number available in the numerical proportion series. This forms four streams of note durations as follows:

Ex.140

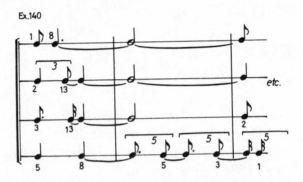

The series (as shown in Ex. 23) is then applied to these streams of duration values, beginning with A = ♪ , and then continuing to follow the path of the numerical series. This provides the following basic musical structure:

Ex.141

This structure is then freely adapted for eight-part choir as follows:

Ex.142   Luigi Nono : *Il Canto Sospeso*

This first procedure is then repeated until the numerical series and its retrograde have been used ten times. This recurring structure gives music which has only a slight ebb and flow of tension. At almost every point there are always at least two long sustaining notes, while groups of shorter notes are spread more or less evenly throughout the structure. This produces continuity in the musical flow, ideally suited to the 'narrative' nature of the words, which require no points of tension-climax or decline.

On the other hand, the second part of this movement (i.e. the last sixteen bars) demands more dramatic treatment and therefore a different structure. The structure just described may be called a 'perpetual' structure, as like a perpetual canon, it could continue over any suitable time-period. The one now to be described is a 'finite' structure, as it is complete within itself.

In this second, 'dramatic' structure, the words demand a growing rhythmic movement and then its dispersion, so a mirror pattern is used. Again the four basic duration values are used as previously, but now each duration value is multiplied by numbers in the order 13 8 5 3 2 1/1 2 3 5 8 13 to produce *horizontal* successions of note values.

Naturally this results in note values which at first are long-drawn-out, then precipitate rapidly to a culmination, and then distend again. Obviously, when the smaller basic durations are multiplied by the numerical series, shorter phrases will result than in the case of the larger duration values, and to increase the sense of precipitation and distention the composer has built them round the centre of the mirror pattern as follows:

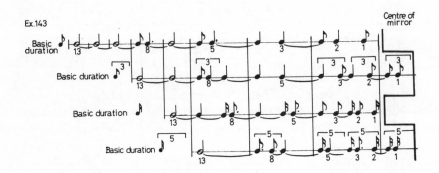

The above design is only half the structure, the 'precipitating' section. The rest mirrors this except for the slight irregularity caused by the delayed entries of basic durations ♪³⌐ and ♪⁵⌐

Again the twelve-note series is applied to this structure by the horizontal-vertical method, so that as each note occurs in time, so is it allotted the next available note from the series. That is, the note series is not used horizontally in each voice part or each succession of basic durations, but according to the order of occurrence of each sound in order of time.

This then provides the following basic musical structure:

The final version (in eight parts) of the first half of this mirror structure
is as follows:

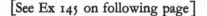

[See Ex 145 on following page]

It will be seen that successions of notes of the same basic duration value
are seldom allotted to one voice only, but are divided up between voices
entirely as the composer desires. Freedom in dividing up an essentially
four-part structure in this pointilliste manner has been the composer's chief
tool in shaping recalcitrant material into a powerfully expressive form.
This is not therefore an example of 'total organization', for the composer's
free choice of registers and dynamics contribute largely towards the formation of his own very personal idiom, and have not been determined by
computational means. The composer's choice of structures has determined
the general musical patterns, but their final shaping is a result of his own
artistry and musical intuition.

2. Rhythmic Cell Constructions

The organization of rhythmic structures through the use of pre-
established rhythmic cells is naturally only an extension of classical principles. But whereas Beethoven would construct a whole movement (such
as the first movement of the Pastoral Symphony) mainly through the
repetition of one or two simple cells, with other more loosely defined
accompanying material, we are dealing here with more complex constructions which use exclusively a definite quantity of material, varied and
combined in every possible way.

Ex. 145

A few basic rhythms are chosen, preferably of 'non-classical' formation, such as the following five rhythms and their retrogrades which constitute the main material in the second movement of my Concerto for Five Instruments and Percussion:

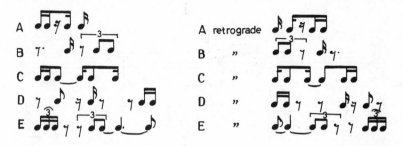

Not only can the five rhythms be used in original and retrograde forms, but each form can be either augmented or diminished by using longer or shorter duration values. For instance, rhythm A can be augmented or diminished as follows:

A augmented: ♩♩♪ ♪ ♪♪♪ ♪   or   ♪♪♪ ♪ ♪♪♪ ♪   etc.
A diminished: ♪♪♪ ♪ ♪♪♪ ♪·   or   ♪♪♪ ♪ ♪♪♪ ♪   etc.

Naturally if slow, tranquil movement is required, augmentations will be used, and if agitated, rapid movement is needed, the rhythms will have diminished values. A more complex structure can be formed by combining rhythms of both augmented, normal, and diminished values, and so on. The variations are infinite, but the important factor is that the rhythms and their variants must conform to some pre-established plan, which will guarantee a specific emotive result. The music must have well-planned periods of repose, intensification, climax, and decline. All these can be achieved with certainty by increasing or diminishing the movement, by intensifying or thinning-off the density of structure and by the use of silences. Naturally dynamics, orchestral colour, and harmonic character will also play an important part.

As an example of the application of this system, here are the first few bars of a section from the Concerto which features the vibraphone and harp almost exclusively:

As will be seen, the vibraphone plays rhythms A, B and E and the harp rhythms C and D, all in their 'original' form and at normal duration values. This is the beginning of a twenty-five bar 'exposition' section in which each instrument plays all five rhythms and their retrogrades in the following order:

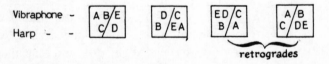

Each instrument therefore plays every basic rhythm and its retrograde. The diagonal line in each 'square' denotes a period of silence and the three gaps between the 'squares' are filled in with interpolations by the flute and clarinet. The rest of the movement then continues with various combinations of this basic material.

It will be observed from Ex. 146 that considerable freedom is preserved in many compositional factors in order to obtain a satisfactory artistic result. The rhythms do not follow each other to produce a continuous discourse. Sometimes two rhythms overlap, sometimes they are separated by silences. Dynamics are used quite freely, and notes are used singly or in combination, to produce continually varied patterns.

This and similar methods of construction can yield very fruitful results, as long as our critical and imaginative faculties are constantly vigilant, for it is naturally essential that the 'system' remains only a means towards self-expression and does not become an end in itself.

RHYTHMIC CONSTRUCTION THROUGH THE SERIES

So far, we have considered only the formation of rhythmic structures determined by means which are external to the series itself, that is, by using pre-determined numerical or rhythmic-cell proportions. Even before 1950, however, compositions were being written in which the series itself was made to dictate rhythmic figurations. Many methods are possible. One of the most simple procedures is that of making the duration of each note proportional to the size of the interval which separates it from the next sound. For instance, if a basic duration value of a semiquaver is assumed for each semitone in intervals, then a series which begins with the notes CF♯DE♭A♭ could form the following patterns:

Ex.147

If, however, the basic duration is made a quaver or longer, the music can be made to move more slowly, or if the basic duration is reduced to a demisemiquaver, the movement will be rapid. If in calculating durations all intervals (however large) are inverted so as to be calculated according to their smallest equivalent form (i.e. within the diminished fifth), notes will follow each other rapidly. If they are calculated as within the octave, or according to wider spans, sounds will be more spaced out. This is a simple means of creating movement (and tension) or more static situations (and relaxation). If chordal groups are formed, then the chord can have a duration equal to the total value of all the intervals it contains. This method is illustrated in the following example from Camillo Togni's *Ricerca* Op. 36:

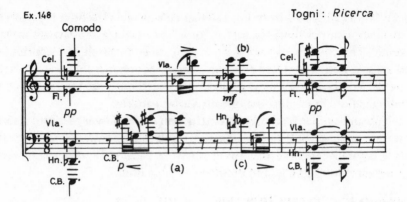

The series used is a chromatic scale of semitones beginning on C. As the basic duration value for each semitone is a semiquaver, the first six-note chord is equal to $6\times \flat = \flat$,. According to the nature of the series, every single note which follows will therefore be a semiquaver, every two-note chord will be a quaver, and so on. However, it will be seen that Togni has allowed himself considerable liberty in breaking the rigidity of the system, for at 'a' and 'b' the two-note chords are prolonged, while at 'c' there is again a slight 'irregularity'. He also reserves complete freedom to organize silences, to repeat notes or prolong them, to establish chordal groups whenever he wishes, and to determine the register and dynamics of each sound.

From such early procedures as this, it was only a short step to the 'integral serialism' or 'total organization' which followed, which allowed composers to compute every factor in a musical edifice. A chain of permutations of a series of notes could determine the note-order of the whole composition. Further chains of permutations of numerical series designed the rhythmic configurations, the note-groupings (chords), the length of silences, and so on. Even note registers, dynamics, instrumentation, and metronomic tempo were determined by some serial process, and in many cases, works of considerable poetic value resulted. However, we can now see that the poetry in this music was produced in spite of the systems and not through their use. The systems had to be moulded skilfully to yield good fruit, and if a composer did not have complete knowledge and control of every compositional factor, the results were merely negative.

Though integral serialism has no virtue in itself, it has served to create a new musical language, rich in possibilities and of considerable dimensions. Since this new language has reached clear definition, the tendency has been to dispense with constructions and to write the same type of music in a completely free manner. Constructions still have their use. Many composers still remain faithful to them, but it would seem that with the re-emergence of free composition music has leaped forward into a quite higher sphere of poetic expression.

With this reaction against constructivism has also come a reaction against other compositional disciplines, including the use of the series. This last is quite logical for many composers no longer need the series as a formal factor and have reached such command of the total-chromatic that the use of a series is superfluous.

Before leaving this section, we must stress one of the principal results of computational methods—the establishment of metrical suspension as a prominent stylistic factor in contemporary music. The partial liquidation of the 'beat' was already apparent in Webern. But now the elimination of metre has become an essential characteristic of our music. The cause is obvious. Extreme rhythmic complexity has cancelled out the metrical foundation which for centuries has had dominion. Whether we regard the elimination of metre as a liberation from tyranny, or with a sense of loss, is no matter. The simple fact is that music can exist without it, just as much as it can exist without so many other elements which not so long ago seemed completely indispensable. There is no doubt that this situation reflects the influence of many factors, not the least being the phenomenon of Webern, the evolution of electronic music, and the extraordinary world we live in.

IMPROVISATION

As an extreme reaction against the calculated definition of totally organized music, some composers have resorted to various kinds of improvisation. But perhaps the revival of improvisation (or 'aleatory' music) is not merely a reaction against extreme organization, it may be a consequence of it. For one of the chief characteristics of computational music or 'integral serialism' is that however highly organized the structures may be, there is no audible evidence of their existence. However diverse the structures may be, music written with complex systems not only has the same general ethos, but also a curiously *extempore* character. It has not been an illogical step, therefore, for composers to reproduce this same extempore quality by the direct means of improvisation, improvisation, let it be understood, which is confined within well-defined stylistic boundaries. These are naturally the use of the total-chromatic, irregular rhythmic configuration, the elimination of metre, etc.

However, if the composer is to retain his status and identity as a creator, even those compositions which are destined to be the subject-matter for improvisation must have some given scheme. Though allowing the performer latitude to improvise within certain defined limits, the composer must still have some control of the main musical events and of the subject matter used. But compositions of this type reveal wide variances of attitude, even in the works of a single composer. Sometimes the music is written out with considerable definition, at others the composition is little more than a design, a graphic representation which can have little precise musical significance.

An example of the former, well-defined type of composition, is Stockhausen's No. 7 *Klavierstück* XI. This consists of nineteen pieces of piano music printed on a single large page. Each piece is absolutely precise as to the notes and rhythms used, but the performer is left free choice in the ordering of the pieces, and considerable latitude as to tempo and dynamics. (Though there are many 'instructions for performance', this is the general gist of the story.) The following example of one of the shorter sections shows the considerable complexity of this music and the definition with which it was written:

Ex: 149   Stockhausen: No 7 Klavierstück XI

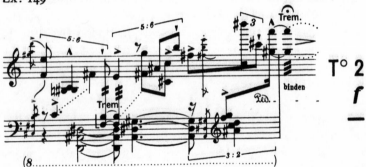

As can be seen, the amount of real improvisation required from the performer is minimal. His capacity for genuine musical invention is hardly tested—in fact the music is still essentially Stockhausen's own creation. A number of compositions for instrumental groups reveal the same characteristics. For instance, in such works as Bo Nilsson's *Reaktionen* for four percussion players (see Ex. 121 for part of this music), the instrumental parts are fairly definite and consist of four musical sections forming a 'canon'. That is, each player begins in a different section, completes that section in his own time, and then the process is repeated 'until the music has reached a playing time of ten minutes'. Naturally many of the results are completely fortuitous, in fact this 'chance' element is deliberately cultivated. The same is true of Nilsson's *Zwanzig Gruppen* for piccolo, oboe, and clarinet. Each instrumentalist has twenty short musical sections in his part, to be played in any order, regardless of the order chosen by other players, so that though each part may be accurately played, the total result is unpredictable. Again the real situation is that very little improvisation is done by the players, the real improvisatory element lies in the chance combination of parts.

On the other hand, other works call for genuine improvisation from the performer. But the amount of musical material given for improvisation varies considerably. Sometimes a large quantity of basic material is given, at others there is only a suggestion of certain musical formations existing as subsidiary elements in a graphic design, while in extreme cases no musical details are given at all—the performer is given a design which bears no relation whatsoever to musical fact.

Henri Pousseur's *Caractères* for piano solo contains twenty-two pages of basic material. The playing instructions are complex both as to the ordering of the segments of materials and as to its interpretation, but much of the actual music given seems little more than ingenuous. There are successions of notes and vague indications as to the speed of execution, no more. If a player has enough imagination to improvise well from this material, he could perhaps do better without it:

Ex. 150   Henri Pousseur: *Caractères*

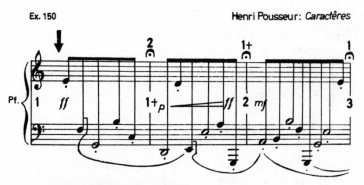

● = normal note, without accidental.
○ = "flattened"note.
Numbers between staves and over the pauses indicate approximate durations of bars and pauses. They do not indicate metre, but time in a "quantitative" sense, '1' being very brief, the others proportionately longer.

A composition which retains a reduced amount of musical indications within a largely graphic scheme is Roman Haubenstock-Ramati's *Mobile for Shakespeare* (Sonnets 53 and 54) for voice and six players. The whole composition is printed on one page, divided into twenty-eight 'areas', grouped into three differently sized rectangles which revolve round the centre. The areas in each rectangle can follow each other in either clockwise or anti-clockwise directions. Each of the twelve areas allotted to the singer corresponds to one line of a sonnet. This is one of the areas allotted to the singer and third percussion player:

Ex: 151   Roman Haubenstock-Ramati: Mobile for Shakespeare

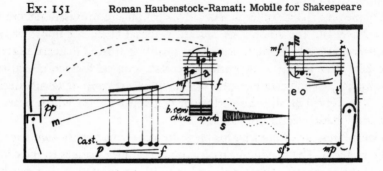

There seems little doubt that a considerable amount of improvisation and imagination is needed to turn such slender suggestions into lyrical song.

As for compositions which are no more than abstract designs, many of these are extremely ingenious and artistic, but can hardly serve as more than a visual stimulus to performers:

Ex : 152   Stockhausen: Zyklus

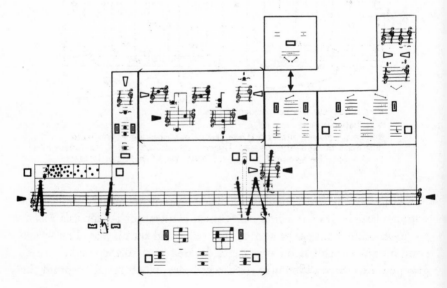

The impeccable quality of improvisation which some players produce in performing these works can only lead us to pay them high tribute and to regard them as true creators in their own right. Fortunately such players do exist. They have great skill, imagination, and creative ability, and it is their excellence which has made this new venture produce aesthetic results of indisputable value and importance in musical history.

Unquestionably, the revival of improvisation is to be welcomed. It has already given fruitful results and will encourage considerable advances in instrumental techniques. It has certainly caused a swing back to spontaneous, 'inspired' expressions, which are welcome enough after a period of extreme cerebralism. But there is little doubt that it constitutes only a minor episode in music's development and that the real future still lies in the hands of the composer who creates entirely definitive works, in which every detail is committed to paper in a complete and unequivocal manner.

16. THE STYLE OF FREE ATONALISM AND FREE TWELVE-NOTE COMPOSITION

The Style of Free Atonalism. Free Twelve-Note Composition.

Though free twelve-note composition has only developed in recent years as a result of serialism, many important aspects of this technique already existed in the style of 'free atonalism' evolved in the few years prior to World War I. In retrospect we can now see that the past fifty years have witnessed a full cycle of musical development. The style of free atonalism was first evolved, then it was rationalized in serialism. After a period of interruption (due to totalitarian rule and World War II) serialism was further evolved, reached a period of maximum rationalization (integral serialism) and then, as a liberating process, free twelve-note composition was introduced, completing the cycle and reviving aspects of the style of free atonalism in a state of full evolution. This is an over-simplification of musical history and ignores many facets of musical development, but it is certain that the future will regard serialism as a phase of development between the style of free atonalism and music written after the experience of integral serialism, in a free twelve-note style.

Before discussing this latter type of non-serial music, however, it is necessary to go back fifty years. Not only have we the moral obligation to study those musical prototypes which originated the whole subject-matter of this book, but we must also discover the main principles of this style of free atonalism, find out its relationship with serialism and observe where the two techniques differ. As a consequence of this study, our final consideration of free twelve-note composition will be simplified and abbreviated and we will have the satisfaction of having considered the whole subject in historical perspective.

THE STYLE OF FREE ATONALISM

Every musical development is the result of exterior forces which dictate aesthetic change. These forces may be social, political, ideological, or religious factors, which, demanding a mutation in artistic expression, necessitate also changes and evolutions in compositional techniques. The style of free atonalism was evolved to fulfil the ideals of the expressionist movement, which in turn resulted from major social and idealogical issues in Germany and Austria around the turn of this century.

To discuss the origins of a major musical style without considering the aesthetic forces which caused its evolution is certainly illogical. Unfortunately, as this book deals with techniques and not with history and aesthetics, we cannot digress on the fascinating story of the expressionist movement, but must confine our observations to matters of compositional technique.

From a purely technical point of view the aims of the creators of the style of free atonalism can be summarized in one main principle—that of creating a musical language which was far removed from tradition. Different composers pursued this ideal to different lengths. As we shall see, Webern was much more radical in his pursuit of this objective than Schoenberg. For the moment it is premature to detail the technical results of their work. It is sufficient to say that their main objective lay in the creation of an atonal language and in so changing melodic and rhythmic patterns that the general musical result was far removed from the ethos of classical music.

In our examination of technical aspects of the style of free atonalism we will confine ourselves to two representative works—Schoenberg's Six Little Piano Pieces, Op. 19 (1911) and Webern's Six Bagatelles for String Quartet, Op. 9 (1913). Both works were written shortly before World War I and consist of a succession of aphoristic pieces in the expressionist manner. Our analysis will be particularly directed towards ascertaining the degrees of atonality created, the relationship (or otherwise) of melodic shapes and rhythmic patterns with traditional archetypes and considering how the examples anticipate serial usage. To assist us in this latter factor, each example will be accompanied by a separated stave illustrating the note-order progression, as if the music were derived from twelve-note series.

We will begin with the fourth piece of Schoenberg's Opus 19, which being mostly in one part only, offers us a particularly clear example:

Ex. 153   Schoenberg: *Six Little Piano Pieces,* Op.19

(all repeated notes are transposed to the same register)

The first seven notes of the melody (as far as the A in bar 2) are all prominent notes in the scale of B♭ minor and the triadic structure underlying the design reinforces the impression of that tonality. Beginning on the A in bar 2, the melody then comprises six notes in A major and then four in a 'white key' tonal zone (C major, F major, D minor, etc.). These latter are then sharply contradicted (bar 4) with three notes in the 'black key' zone of tonalities. Throughout the melody, a number of notes give the impression of being substitution or auxiliary notes (these are marked with an 'x'), others of being passing notes (e.g. the F♯ in bar 3, G♯ in bar 4, etc.). So far, it would seem that the melody moves through various contrasting tonalities and that the use of triadic and scalic patterns, as well as auxiliary notes and passing notes, confirms the close relationship of this melody with traditional note-patterns.

At points where chords are formed, it would at first seem that tonal suggestions are disrupted, but on analysis, we find that the chord in bar 2 (B–F) functions as a pivot chord, the F belonging to the first melodic tonal zone of B♭ minor, the B♮ to the second zone of A major. In bar 4, especially through the use of the sustaining pedal, a complex chord is built up comprising seven different notes. This chord is particularly obscure through dissonance in the lower register, but if the three lowest notes (DFG) are transposed into the octave above middle C, it will be seen that the chord is no other than that of C minor seventh, with major seventh, ninth and eleventh (BDF). The harmonic background of these chords is therefore not atonal.

Turning to the rhythmic design of the melody, this comprises two phrases, the first of 'double dotted' rhythms, the second of flowing semi-quavers, which are completely classical in outline and need no further comment. However, the rest of this piece makes no further use of this material, every melodic phrase being of different pattern, though classical in shape.

Considering the note-order of this example with a view to assessing its anticipations of serialism, we find that a series can only be formed by including the twenty notes up to G♯ in bar 4 (all black notes in the separate stave indicate repeated notes). We can conclude that though Schoenberg used all twelve notes of the total-chromatic within a fairly short span, certain prominent note repetitions and the presence of tonal note-group-ings indicate that he had no conception here of serial principles, nor any intention of adhering to total-chromatic note-orders.

Our next example, the first piece of Schoenberg's Op. 19, is slightly more complex:

Ex. 154   Schoenberg : *Six Little Piano Pieces*, Op.19

Taking the melodic aspect first, we find this to be divided into two phrases of completely classical shape. In fact there is nothing about this melody which could not have come from the pen of Mendelssohn. However, like the fourth piece of Op. 19, this piece makes no further use of these phrases, but proceeds with constantly changing melodic fragments.

Though the rhythms of the melody are quite classical, those of the accompaniment have a different character. They are fragmentary and inconclusive, giving the music the intangible quality of many expressionist compositions.

The harmony again seems to be directed towards atonal fields. but this is largely caused by the inclusion of non-essential and auxiliary notes. It is evident from the outset that much of the harmonic construction is triadic in conception. The first note-group is the chord of A minor, with the major seventh and ninth and the added complication of a dissonant auxiliary note (G♮). In the last half of bar 1 the presence of seventh, ninth, and auxiliary notes obscures a closely related key—E minor. This tonality persists throughout bar 2 to the end of the example, again obscured by the same means. That the whole passage is really in E minor can be easily proved by adding a chord of E minor in root position after playing through the example. It will be perceived that this E minor chord has an indisputable sense of 'tonic' and reveals itself as the basic tonality of the whole passage and not just as a fugitive tonal gesture. A further proof may be obtained by playing through the example, omitting the more tonally-disruptive elements and letting the basic key emerge. It is surprising how few notes need to be suppressed or resolved to do this.

We are therefore dealing here not with atonality, but only with obscured tonality. The same is true of all the pieces in Schoenberg's Op. 19, except the last, which being based on harmony of fourths, presents the characteristics of that technique.

As for the note-order of this example, it will be seen that twenty-four notes occur before Schoenberg used all twelve notes of the chromatic scale. As the first seven notes are all different, it would seem that he set out to use a fairly chromatic technique, but in reality these seven notes all belong to the same tonality—E (major or minor), The remaining five notes of the chromatic scale then only appear singly, separated by numerous repetitions of previous notes. Of the twelve repetitions of previous notes it will be seen that all of them, with one exception (B♭), belong to the tonality of E minor. It is obvious, therefore, that the note-order of this piece in no way anticipates serial principles, nor adheres to the concepts of totally-chromatic writing.

It would be pointless to present further examples of Schoenberg's Opus 19, for the same story would emerge again and again.

Turning to Webern's Six Bagatelles for String Quartet, Op. 9, we find a remarkably different state of affairs, contrasting in every aspect with

Schoenberg's pieces. It is sufficient to quote the beginning of the first
movement, as this is technically completely representative of all six:

Ex.155 Webern : *Six Bagatelles for String Quartet*, Op.9

Note-order

Melodically, the piece contains no more than brief phrases, not con-
nected in a classical manner, but with isolated note groups usually spanning over a large intervallic range. The five-note phrase of the first violin
happens to be the longest in this piece and is rarely exceeded in length in
the whole work. Rhythmic designs have little continuity, and throughout
all six pieces there is a considerable degree of that metrical suspension
characteristic of Webern's later serial music. We can therefore conclude
that in melodic and rhythmic aspects, Webern's Opus 9 has little immediate affinity with traditional archetypes and already anticipates the pattern
of serial music of a considerably later period.

From the harmonic point of view, it is obvious that no note-combinations are the result of triadic thinking. No vertical combination of notes in
all six pieces gives the least impression of having originated (as we have
seen with Schoenberg) from a system of obscuring triad harmony.

Webern's approach has been quite different and the best way to understand it is to try to divine his line of thought, which could have been as follows:[1]

Beginning on D (cello) the first step was to eliminate an immediate suggestion of D as tonality by an E♭ (viola). The third step was to choose a note which would further eliminate any tendency of D and E♭ to emerge as components of triadic harmony. If the third note had been F, F♯, G, A, B♭, or B♮ a harmonic group would have been formed which, though dissonant, would have given, in some degree, an impression of tonal harmony. A♭ or C would do so, but to a considerably less extent. Only C♯ or E could be added if the same degree of non-tonality were to be maintained. Webern chose to use C♯ as the third note (Vn. 1).

At this point (bar 2) the C♯, being sustained without the earlier notes, began a new sequence of thought. This C♯ had to have any tonal suggestions eliminated and this was best done by a C♮ or D. As D had already been used, and wishing to preserve a totally-chromatic note-order, Webern therefore chose to contradict C♯ with C♮ (Vn. 2). In order to follow these two notes with a third which again avoided the formation of a tonal group, the ideal choice would have been D or B. D had already been used and was therefore not available. B would have been excellent, but would have continued the same semitonic note sequence as had been previously used. Considering this a weak feature to be avoided, Webern had therefore the alternative of using one of the two notes (G♭ or B♭), which added to C and C♯, would least suggest a tonal group. To use a low B♭ in the second violin at this point would give the impression that the previous C♮ had been forced to 'resolve' downwards by the C♯ in the first violin. Regarding this as an undesirable traditionalism, Webern therefore chose to G♭ in the second violin part.

That Webern chose to conclude the second violin phrase with an A♭ (bar 2) seems at first to go against his principle of avoiding tonal associations, for the notes in this phrase (C, G♭ and A♭) suggest the chord of A♭ seventh. But any such impression was carefully eliminated in the viola part by introducing an A♮ and B 'ostinato' figure.

From this point the viola part (bar 2) may be regarded (from a harmonic point of view) as two notes (A and B) sustained over the second and third beats of the bar. We must now consider that having used eight notes of the total-chromatic, Webern only had the choice of four notes with which to continue (E, F, G, and B♭), if totally-chromatic writing were to

[1]This presumed 'line of thought' is later referred to in this chapter as Webern's 'method' of free atonalism. Unfortunately we have no record of his methods in 1913, but the one suggested here seems almost certain to be correct.

be maintained. Of these, only one, the B♭, creates a really atonal rapport with the viola A and B♮. Webern therefore chose to begin the first violin phrase with B♭, after which he could safely follow on with E and F providing the note to be introduced by the cello did not confirm tonal associations between the first violin (E and F) and the viola (A and B).

This is where a revealing event occurred. In his obvious endeavour to use all twelve notes of the chromatic scale before repeating any of them, Webern was here faced with a dilemma. For at the end of bar 2 (excluding the cello part) Webern had already used eleven notes of the total-chromatic and only G remained. To use this G in the cello part would have been catastrophic—there should be no reason to say why! Webern therefore chose to give the cello a note (F♯) which contradicted the tonal suggestions in the upper parts and delayed the use of G until the first beat of bar 3 in the first violin part.

In this procedure Webern anticipated a very characteristic serial practice (serial manipulation), and throughout all six movements we find the same kind of event recurring again and again.

At this point, Webern had used the whole total-chromatic and we can cease our analysis, which, though somewhat laborious, has thrown light on a harmonic practice very different from Schoenberg's technique of obscuring tonalities.

We can conclude that it was Webern's endeavour not only to use the total-chromatic consistently and continuously (for all movements of Opus 9 demonstrate the same technique), but to eliminate deliberately all tonal suggestions, note by note, as they occurred. The discourse is consistently atonal. Furthermore, the same degree of atonality is carefully preserved, particularly by semitonic 'contradictions' of any notewhich would otherwise emerge as a key centre.

Finally, we will now consider the note-order of this example and compare it with serial usage. From the note-order stave we can see that, except for the repeated F♯ (which we know is fully justified) the note-order adheres closely with serial ideals. There is only one note-group which has tonal associations (CG♭A♭) and the characteristic notes of this group are contradicted by the adjacent C♯ and A♮.

In other movements, also, the note-orders are quite serial in character. In the beginnings of three other movements, eleven different notes occur before any repetition takes place. 'Tonal' note-groups are very rare and in any case are carefully contradicted in the musical context. In fact, the only aspect of serial note-orderings which is absent, is that there is no common series of notes throughout the work.

To sum up, our examination of these two works reveals a considerable divergence of technique between two of the principal masters of the style of free atonalism.

While Schoenberg's melodic phrases and rhythms recall classical models, those of Webern do not. While Schoenberg's harmony is directed towards the atonal plane by obscuring triadic note-formations of conventional origin, Webern's approach to atonality is through a calculated elimination of tonality by avoiding all triadic or other tonal associations. Finally, while Schoenberg does not consistently use the total-chromatic, Webern uses this to the fullest possible degree and the note-orders of his work have many affinities with serial music.

Naturally this strong divergence in technique results in music of strongly different character and, in passing, we may mention that even after both composers adopted the serial method of composition, their music still demonstrated the same contrasting characteristics. Their use of serialism did not change their basic compositional approach, but only served to rationalize their methods.

FREE TWELVE-NOTE COMPOSITION

The free twelve-note composition which in recent years has followed the extreme radicalism of integral serialism and demonstrates some composers' inclinations to return to a freer method of working, has little in common with Schoenberg's early style of free atonalism, but is closely aligned in many procedures with Webern's practice in that style. In fact, the basic compositional method is virtually identical, if considerably more developed and evolved.

There is the same consistent use of the total-chromatic. No note is repeated within each cycle of the twelve different semitones unless there is some valid reason (as we have just observed in Webern's Opus 9). There is no common series used, but each recurrence of the twelve semitones is, as it were, a self-contained series with its note-order suggested by the immediate necessities of that particular musical section.

As for the harmonic language, Webern's method is followed precisely. Each note-group or sequence of notes is formed so as to create the exact degree of atonality required, eliminating triadic formations and classical tonal suggestions. However, harmony now tends to a greater complexity than that in Webern's Opus 9, through the use of dense harmonic textures and the superimposition of various strata of sound on each other.

In free twelve-note composition, the note-orders are therefore completely free, but the total-chromatic is used as consistently as is practical, avoiding note repetitions where possible within each recurrence or 'cycle' of the twelve semitones other than those demanded by the musical context. Furthermore, the note-order is designed to eliminate tonal note-groups, in precisely the same way as we have observed in the construction of an 'atonal' series. In the harmonic field, we find a calculated elimination of tonalities and the creation of an atonal norm built only on tension relationships.

There is, however, an alternative to Webern's method of working in free atonalism which should be illustrated at this point. Webern's method of working[2] involves a continuous calculation of note-relationships (vertically) as each new note is introduced. Not only is this a slow process, but the attention is inevitably concentrated mostly on the *vertical* relationships, so that the *horizontal* flow of each part over an adequate period tends to be relegated to secondary considerations. The horizontal flow of each part inevitably suffers in consequence.

We wish to indicate an alternative method in which the horizontal flow of important parts may be first arranged, and the vertical (harmonic) combination of parts controlled afterwards by the addition of another voice. This makes for quicker working and a better horizontal line in each part. We will first show how a *lower* part can control any harmonic situation with facility and create harmony of either tense or relaxed qualities at will. Then we will illustrate the same procedure in an upper part.

To illustrate the method of working, we will add a lower part to Exx. 52 and 54, the first example comprising groups of *consonant* two-note intervals, the second of *dissonant* two-note intervals. Both examples use the total-chromatic, in fact the first of these examples was derived from strict serial usage (the 'O' version of the series in Webern's Op. 23). Though in free twelve-note composition we would naturally not use a series, we have deliberately chosen to use Ex. 52 here in order to illustrate the possibility of adding a free part to other parts derived from a series, as referred to at the end of Chapter 8.

As all the intervals in Ex. 52 are consonant (except the second which is a neutral tritone) we will first show how the addition of a suitable lower part can neutralize the consonances and produce an effect of *mild* tension throughout:

[2]To be more correct—what we have presumed to be Webern's method.

Ex.156

consonances

2c	1c	2c		1c
1m	1n	1m ————————		1n
	1m			1m

Lower part creates harmony of mild tensions.

As every chord (except the second and last) is made up of two consonances and one mild dissonance, the harmonic flow is of evenly mild tension. The second and last chords, formed of one consonance, one neutral tritone and one mild dissonance, have a very similar degree of tension to the other chords and merge well with them. All the notes of the 'free' part are different, thus corresponding with a consistent use of the total-chromatic and avoiding note fatigue. False relations of the octave are avoided.

We will now add a bass to the consonant upper parts which will produce harmony of *strong* tension:

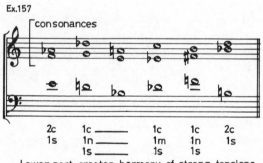

Ex.157

consonances

2c	1c ———	1c	1c	2c
1s	1n ———	1m	1n	1s
	1s ———	1s	1s	

Lower part creates harmony of strong tensions.

The strong tension has been maintained on a fairly even scale by introducing a sharp dissonance (semitone or its inversion) in each chord. However, some variety of tension has been introduced. The first and last chords are mildest in tension (two consonances and one sharp dissonance). The remainder all comprise one consonance, one neutral interval and one sharp dissonance except the fourth chord (one consonance, one mild dissonance and one sharp dissonance). The harmonic tension therefore increases towards the fourth chord and then decreases to the same scale as the beginning.

Suppose a change from complete consonance to strong tension were needed, this could be produced as follows:

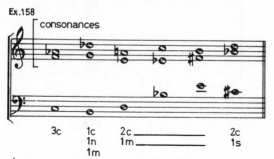

Ex.158

```
consonances
```

3c   1c   2c _____ 2c
      1n   1m _____ 1s
      1m

Lower part creates movement from consonance to strong tension.

After the complete consonance of the first chord, one mild dissonance is introduced in the succeeding chords, until a sharp dissonance is reached in the final chord. Obviously, a reverse movement from strong tension to relaxation could be achieved just as easily by first introducing strong dissonances and then moving towards greater consonance.

We will now test the effect of adding a lower part to *dissonant* intervals. Using the 'all dissonant' intervals of Ex. 54 we will turn the harmony into a more consonant, relaxed channel by the addition of a lower part which is consonant with *both* notes on the upper stave:

Ex.159

```
dissonances
```

2c   2c   2c   2c   2c   2c
1m   1s   1m   1s   1n   1m

Lower part disperses tension in upper parts.

It is a simple matter to add a lower part which will *add* to the tension in the upper parts:

Ex.160

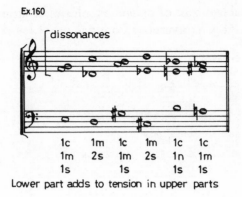

dissonances

1c	1m	1c	1m	1c	1c
1m	2s	1m	2s	1n	1m
1s		1s		1s	1s

Lower part adds to tension in upper parts

The lower part is always at a distance of a semitone (or its inversion) from one note in the upper parts.

By now it should be obvious that whatever the tension relationship between two parts, a third part can be added below them which can substantially alter the harmonic effect produced by the two parts alone. In fact a lower 'free' part can control harmonic situations completely. The same is true even with a greater number of parts. We do not wish to labour the issue and investigate the matter at great length, it is sufficient to show one example. With the following 'harshly dissonant' chord in the upper stave, there are four alternative bass notes (C B F or B♭) which will tend (in various degrees) to produce an effect of greater consonance, while there are four other alternative bass notes (A♭ F♯ E and C♯) which increase the effect of tension:

Ex.161

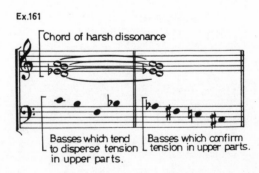

Chord of harsh dissonance

Basses which tend to disperse tension in upper parts.   Basses which confirm tension in upper parts.

So far we have only dealt with the addition of a free *lower* part. The addition of an *upper* part achieves just the same kind of harmonic control, though it has a slightly less potent degree of influence. In the following examples the 'all consonant' succession of two-part chords in Ex. 52 is given a considerable degree of tension by adding an upper part which is always a semitone (or its inversion) from one of the lower parts:

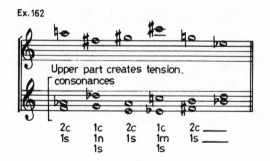

Ex. 162

Upper part creates tension.

or alternatively the 'all dissonant' group in Ex. 54 is made more consonant by adding an upper part which is consonant with both lower notes:

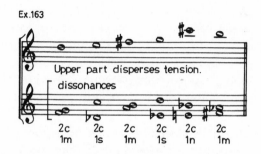

Ex. 163

Upper part disperses tension.

But in music of more than three parts, an added upper part ceases to have the same power of harmonic control as an added lower part, because inevitably the most potent harmonic influences are created in the lower regions of chords. It is therefore best, in music of many parts, to control the harmonic equilibrium with a lower part wherever possible, rather than with an upper part.

So far, however, we have only illustrated this method of tension control in free twelve-note composition (or in a free form of serialism) with chords in which all the notes occur simultaneously. In actual practice, this rarely happens over anything but limited musical periods. It is much more common to find the 'overlapping' of notes. One part may be sustained while another moves over two or more notes, as in the upper stave of the following example. Here the upper parts move simultaneously only at two points, at all others they overlap. Nevertheless, it has been quite easy to add a lower part which at all points controls the tension flow. In fact, to show how tension can be controlled, two alternative bass parts have been given, one which gives constantly relaxed harmony (bass 'a') and one which maintains a uniformly moderate tension (bass 'b'):

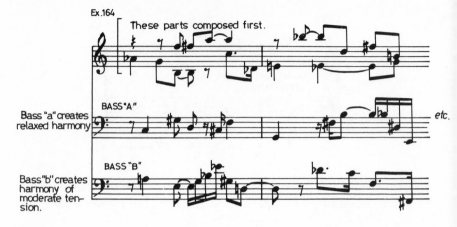

In bass 'a', a few 'tonal' triads have been deliberately included to show that, if need be, the harmony can be channelled into tonal spheres if desired, so great is the degree of harmonic control with this method. In the above example, both upper parts were composed first, using between them all twelve notes before repeating any note. The bass was then added, again using the total-chromatic and avoiding octaves or false relations of the octave.

In actual practice it is therefore possible to compose two or more horizontal parts first (those which are probably the most important part of the musical discourse) and later add a further free part above or below these which will control the harmonic tension flow satisfactorily. In this way, a better horizontal flow of parts should be possible than if Webern's method of free atonalism were used. Furthermore, the process of composition is made easier and good results obtained more quickly. Inevitably, parts composed first will use the total-chromatic continuously, and the part added later will use all twelve notes systematically, avoiding octaves and false relations of the octave. The process is therefore not unlike the simultaneous use of two different serial forms, except that the same note-sequences do not recur, as in serial practice.

So far, our discussion of free twelve-note composition has concentrated on establishing methods of organizing horizontal note successions and their vertical combinations. These methods provide a technique which can replace serial usage in the creation of melody, harmony and counterpoint. But we have not discussed other important factors such as form and style. This is because free twelve-note composition does not necessarily require forms and styles of its own which do not already exist in serial music. On the contrary, free twelve-note composition can be adapted to any of the styles and forms of serial music, except those where formal designs originate from the series itself, as in integral serialism.

It would be wrong, at this point, to indicate any specific forms and styles for free twelve-note composition. But we must record that, as free twelve-note composition has followed the phase of integral serialism, the general tendency so far has been to continue the general stylistic features of that movement, without resorting to serialism or to the pre-determined structures derived from serial usage. There is the same complex rhythmic figuration, the same obscuring of metre and general elimination of classical musical characteristics. But as the music (with free twelve-note usage) is freely conceived, rather than calculated by arbitrary methods, it tends to be more spirited and demonstrates greater flights of fantasy. But as the formal structures of integral serialism are no longer present, composers have had to choose a formal method which tends to give similar results to the structures of integral serialism. As these structures, despite their considerable formal organization, are not audibly recognizable, but tend to give a free, extempore quality to the music it has been quite logical that composers using free twelve-note composition have adopted the nearest formal equivalent—that is, 'free' forms, as described in Chapter 10.

This is free twelve-note composition in its most extreme form—that style which has developed as a consequence of, and perhaps as a reaction against, the constructivism of integral serialism. But this is by no means the whole picture. For free twelve-note composition can be used as a technical basis for writing music in all the varied styles to which serialism has been adapted. There is absolutely no reason why such serial works as Stravinsky's *Threni*, Schoenberg's *Moses and Aaron*, Webern's Symphony Op. 21, or Berg's *Lulu*, could not have been written in a free style, without using any series. The only reason which can be advanced is that the works would lack 'serial unity'. But as composers usually strive to avoid too-obvious serial relationships and aim for thematic variety rather than constancy, the continuous recurrence of the series is rarely audible and therefore 'serial unity' is often enough a chimera of questionable practical value. The only kind of audible unity a series can provide is one of thematic character and if such thematic unity is needed, it can easily be provided through free composition, rather than by the roundabout method of serial practice.

The various styles of serial music we have discussed in this book result from different methods of working, the use of different forms, varying degrees of harmonic tension (to conform with specific tonal or atonal requirements), various ways of forming melody, counterpoint, textures, and so on. In all cases, we have found that the series has to be made to conform with linguistic requirements. It must not dictate the music itself (except in integral serialism) but has to be manipulated and skilfully handled to form every melodic phrase, every note-combination, every tension-relationship. There is no reason whatsoever why such a cumbersome method should not be abandoned, and the same music written freely, without the strictures of serialism.

However skilfully we may work, the series is in constant opposition to our uninhibited imagination. Our imagination may at first suggest a certain succession of sounds, but the series dictates a different group of notes. We have therefore to make the series conform with what our imagination demands, or alter what we first thought of to suit what is available in the series. This kind of compromise is happening ceaselessly and if we find our mental images inhibited by serial strictures, we would do much better to follow a free method of composition. But our task would not be easy and it can only be accomplished after all the musical values thrown up by serialism have been completely absorbed. Every 'free' method will, in fact, not be free, but will have its own disciplines. For music which is to have consistency of style, technique, and character, must inevitably be the result of well-formed principles—principles resulting from the composer's evaluation of every aspect of technique, his choice of certain factors, his rejection of others. It is necessary to know the value of every sound, the implications of every interval, the meaning of every note-combination. Above all, it is necessary to be able to think instinctively in terms of total-chromaticism and without the facilitation of Schoenberg's twelve-note series or Hauer's tropes, this is no easy task.

Only the most bigoted partisan of serialism could deny that it is more ideal to compose relatively freely than through a restrictive method. Our aim should be to conquer every facet of technique and then strike out boldly along the path suggested by our uninhibited imagination. It may be an arduous route, we may frequently have to fall back on the structures of serialism, but in the end our work will be authentic, truly creative, and without the dross of functional systems.

But there is no short cut to the technique of free twelve-note composition. It can only be attempted after the discipline of serialism has been completely absorbed, when the mind instinctively thinks in terms of total-chromaticism and when new self-imposed disciplines can be evolved. This is why the main body of this book is devoted to serialism, the only effective method available to us at the moment for our exploration of a vast uncharted territory, the confines of which are still unknown and the ways and byeways still only dimly perceived.

194

EXERCISES

CHAPTERS 2, 3 and 4. VARIOUS KINDS OF SERIES AND THEIR
DERIVED FORMS (PAGES 4-22)

1. Beginning with the notes G, F♯ and A, continue with nine different
   notes to produce (a) a tonal series, (b) an atonal series, (c) a symmetrical
   series, (d) an all-interval series, (e) a symmetrical all-interval series.
2. Write the derived forms of the various series in the previous question.

CHAPTER 5. WRITING MELODY (PAGES 23-34)

1. Complete the series and write a violin melody of 'traditional' type,
   with phrase repetitions and extensions based on segments 'a' and 'b'.

2. Complete the series and continue the following melody for unison
   violins, about 16 bars in all. The melody must be of a lyrical nature
   (note-groups and/or rhythms may be repeated) and should rise to a
   mild climax and then fall back to pianissimo.

(c.f. the author's *Creation Epic*, finale)

3. Write a vigorous melody for horn, without repeating rhythms or
   note-groups and beginning as follows:

4. Continue the following melody for clarinet, with well-contrasted phrases, in a vigorous 'hungarian' style:

(c.f. the author's *Concerto for five instruments and percussion*)

5. Write a 'scherzino' for piccolo. Do not repeat any rhythms. Use irregular patterns, jagged, jaunty phrase outlines and exploit both the suave and brilliant registers of the instrument.

CHAPTER 6. WRITING IN TWO PARTS (PAGES 35-48)

1. Write a 'serenata' for violin and guitar in the form of melody and accompaniment, continuing the series indicated and beginning as follows:

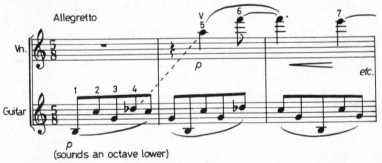

2. Continue the following duo for oboe and bassoon, both parts to be independent but one predominating:

3. Using two independent parts of equal importance, write a fanfare for two trumpets. Use the series of Webern's Op. 23 and its derived forms as shown in Chapter 4:

4. Complete the following *canon at the octave* for piano:

5. Continue the following *canon by inversion* for flute and bassoon:

CHAPTER 7. MUSIC IN SEVERAL PARTS (PAGES 49-60)

1. Using the *horizontal-vertical* method of serial usage applied to the 'O' version only of Webern's series for Op. 23 (cf. Chapter 4), continue the following as a short composition for flute, clarinet, and cello. Use serial manipulation wherever necessary:

2. Write a piece of lively rhythmic character for vibraphone, guitar, and double-bass pizzicato, using 4-note segments (and other segment-forms if desired) of various forms of Webern's series in Op. 23 (cf. Chapter 4). Begin as follows:

3. Re-write the two previous questions using different versions of the series for each instrument. Manipulate the series wherever necessary in order to obtain satisfactory results.

4. Expand the music you have written for Question 1 above into a piece for chamber orchestra. Each of the three instrumental parts you have written may be expanded into numerous parts. Some appropriate phrases may be retained as single-note passages, others may be filled out as chords or varying density. Use the *horizontal-vertical* method of serial

usage in some sections. In others, use derived or transposed forms of the series in each horizontal line.

CHAPTER 8. TWELVE-NOTE HARMONY (PAGES 61-88)

1. Dispose the following three-note groups, each in six different ways, so that by varying the order and register of each note, chords are formed which progress from maximum dissonance to greatest consonance:

$$F \quad G\flat \quad A\flat$$
$$G \quad B\flat \quad B\natural$$
$$D \quad G\sharp \quad A$$

2. Procede as in Question 1, forming eight chords with each of the following four-note groups:

$$E \quad F \quad G\flat \quad A$$
$$D \quad E \quad G\sharp \quad C\sharp$$
$$F \quad G\flat \quad A\flat \quad A\natural$$

3. Similarly, form eight chords with each of the following six-note groups:

$$C \quad D \quad E\flat \quad E\natural \quad F \quad A\flat$$
$$E\flat \quad E\natural \quad F \quad B \quad C \quad D$$
$$G \quad A \quad C \quad E \quad F \quad F\sharp$$

4. Using the series of Webern's Op. 23 (cf. Chapter 4) in any of its derived forms, write three-part harmony disposing the series as follows:
   (a) in strict vertical orderings downwards.
   (b) in strict vertical orderings upwards.
   (c) in serial segments disposed horizontally in each part.

5. Repeat Question 4 but writing four-part harmony.

6. Improve the harmony obtained in Questions 4 and 5 by (a) a free vertical ordering of the two lower parts, (b) a free vertical ordering of all parts in each chord.

7. Using the series for Webern's Op. 23, write four-part harmony using a completely free ordering which will produce:
   (a) conventional chromatic harmony.
   (b) harmony of a moderate degree of tension.
   (c) harmony of a considerable degree of tension.
   (Naturally, free ordering can only mean abandoning serial usage, but here it is suggested that the series is used as a basis for free choice.)

8. Write four-part chords using different forms of the series of Webern's Op. 23 (Chapter 4) *horizontally* in each part. Eliminate all octaves and false relations of the octave and by serial manipulation, create a logical and smooth harmonic flow. Variations in tension–degrees between the chords are desirable, but unpleasant associations of excessive consonance and excessive dissonance should be avoided.

CHAPTER 9. POLYPHONIC WRITING (PAGES 89-100)

1. Using the series indicated, continue the following *canon* for flute and bass clarinet for about 12-16 bars. The consequent (flute) must use the series transposed at the tritone.

2. Write a *canon by inversion* in two parts, for guitar and cello pizzicato, using 'O' and 'I' versions of the series used in Question 1.

3. Continue the following three-part canon, consisting of cello (antecedent), clarinet (transposed consequent), and oboe (inverted consequent). Use 'O', 'O' transposed and 'I' versions of the series in Question 1.

4. Write a piece in 'serenata' style using *canon cancrizans* form, for mandolin and guitar. Use various forms of the series in Question 1 above. Begin and end as follows, using the 'I' version:

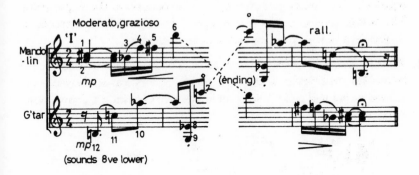

5. Add a free (non-canonic) violin part to the previous question, using serial forms and maintaining a lyrical *cantabile* style.

6. Write a canon by *augmentation* for celesta and harp, the harp to play the celesta part augmented to double the time values. The celesta part must be in mirror form. Using the series in Question 1 above, begin as follows:

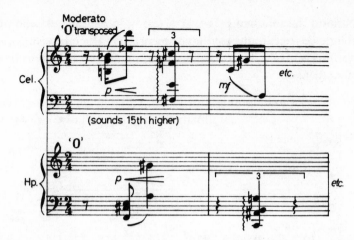

7. Add a 'free' flute part to the above, using serial forms, manipulated where necessary. Adopt a light, agile manner, with rapid arabesques, note repetitions, grace notes, tremolos, etc, to give an elegant, fanciful line.

8. Write a climax for full brass using canonic devices such as augmentation and diminution in order to write music which begins with slow movement, but precipitates rapidly towards a culminating point. Begin with augmentations in the lower parts, then introduce the canon and/or its inversion in normal time values in the middle registers, then finally add diminished consequents in the upper parts. The whole section need only occupy a few bars. Plan the rhythmic designs first before deciding on the note-ordering.

9. Write a *double canon* for string quartet. The principal canon to be between the first violin and viola, the secondary canon between the second violin and cello. Using the series as in Question 1 above, begin as follows:

10. Rewrite any of Questions 1, 2, 3, 6, or 9 as *rhythmic canons*. Imitation should be exact in the rhythmic aspect only. The note-sequences used should be free (though serial) and any suggestion of intervallic imitation avoided.

11. Write a short composition for violin, vibraphone, and bass clarinet in *free counterpoint*, without imitations. Begin as follows, using the series indicated:

12. Expand the number of parts used in the canons in Questions 1, 2, and 4 to produce canons for two keyboard instruments (two pianos, harpsichord and celesta, etc.). The number of parts used in chords may vary, and single-note phrases may be retained where suitable.

13. Rewrite any of the rhythmic canons obtained in Question 10 as a piece for chamber orchestra, expanding the number of parts (in chords) freely.

14. Using the rhythmic designs obtained in Question 11, expand the number of parts to make a short piece for piano and wind ensemble.

CHAPTER 11. VOCAL WRITING (PAGES 112-120)

1. Choose your own words and write a song for solo voice in which the note-orders follow serial patterns. But retain traditional characteristics in other features such as phrase designs, repetitions and over-all form.

2. Set a Shakespeare sonnet for solo voice, avoiding traditional usages to whatever degree you think suitable.

3. Adopt the same procedure as in Question 1, but write for voice and piano accompaniment.

4. Add an accompaniment for small chamber ensemble (e.g. flute, cello, harp, and vibraphone)to the vocal part written in Question 2. The voice part need not have the same continuity, but may be subdivided into a number of sections separated by brief instrumental interludes.

5. Choose your own words and write a song for voice and chamber orchestra, but in composing, 'think out' the vocal line before deciding on the exact accompaniment.

6. Write an *a cappella* chorus for mixed choir on a religious text, using serialism in a renaissance contrapuntal style as in Stravinsky's *Threni*, Dallapiccola's *Canti di Prigionia*, etc.

CHAPTER 12. ORCHESTRATION, TEXTURE AND TONE COLOUR (PAGES 121-138)

1. Orchestrate movements from Dallapiccola's *Quaderno Musicale di Annalibera* (Suvini Zerboni Editions) for piano and compare with the composer's own solutions in his *Variations for Orchestra*.

2. Orchestrate the first and last movements of Schoenberg's *Sechs Kleine Klavierstucke* Op. 19 (Universal Edition) for chamber orchestra.

3. Make a reduction for piano of parts of the first movement of Luigi Nono's *Il Canto Sospeso* (Schott & Co for Ars Viva Verlag).

CHAPTER 14. PERMUTATIONS AND OTHER VARIANTS (PAGES 154-160)

1. Choosing any series you wish, write permutations using any suitable procedure you may care to adopt. Test the results in order to assess the relative suitability (or otherwise) of the various new series formed.

2. Using the permutations arrived at in the previous question, form a 'chain' of four satisfactory permutations which will provide a succession of 48 notes in which no note is repeated at too close an interval (i.e. without at least three or four intervening notes).

1. Write an *a cappella* chorus on a religious text, forming the voice parts from the proportions 2.1.1 and the retrograde 1.1.2. Apply these proportions to various duration values in order to give an ebb and flow of movement. Rests may be of any suitable duration. Write the rhythmic plan of the piece before determining the exact notes through serial methods.

2. Write a short movement for chamber ensemble or orchestra in which as much detail as possible is derived from the numerical proportions 1.2.3.5 and the retrograde 5.3.2.1. Apply these proportions to various duration values in order to determine the place in time of each note. Complete a plan of the rhythmic designs of the piece first, then apply the series by any suitable method in order to determine which notes are to be used at any given point. Try to use the same numerical succession as a principle for the formation of chords, instrumentation and dynamics. Make sure that the plan of the piece will provide a good tension flow, with points of culmination and repose, zones of constant tension (strong or weak), etc.

3. Write a piano piece using the series indicated and using rhythms A, B and C in augmented, diminished and retrograde forms. Dynamics, the formation of chords, the duration of rests between each rhythm, etc., are at your discretion. Begin as follows:

4. Use the following rhythms and their augmentations, diminutions, and retrogrades as the basis of a movement for full orchestra:

The plan for a five-minute movement may be as follows:

(1) A tentative opening (quiet dynamics, tranquil movement, etc.).

(2) A zone of vigorous movement moving to a climax.

(3) A zone of repose.

(4) Similar to (2) but shorter and moving to a greater climax.

(5) A zone of rapid decline.

(6) *either* a period where all tension resolves *or* a rapid, vigorous climax.

Each section of the orchestra (woodwind, horns, brass, percussion, strings, etc.) will use the four rhythms in varied orders and forms and in different ways. Only at points of climax will rhythms overlay each other in all orchestral sections, at most other points the simultaneous use of different rhythms will be much less frequent. Chords may be formed with each rhythm, or single-note phrases, or the number of notes used may vary from moment to moment. Dynamics, rests, instrumentation, note registers, etc., are free.

5. Write a short piece for wind quintet in which every detail is derived from a twelve-note series. Use your own methods for making the note-durations and registers, dynamics, silences and chordal combinations depend on some kind of formula derived from the note series (cf. the *String Quartet* and *Serenata No. 2* of Bruno Maderna, Boulez's *Structures*, etc.).

CHAPTER 16. FREE TWELVE-NOTE COMPOSITION (PAGES 178-194)

1. Add a free part below the following succession of dissonant intervals in order to provide a relatively smooth harmonic flow throughout:

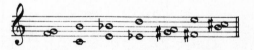

2. Add a free part *above* the intervals in Question 1 which will maintain maximum intervallic tension.

3. Add a free part below the following haphazard succession of consonant and dissonant intervals in order to create chordal progressions which are (1) of relatively uniform mild tension, (2) of uniformly strong tension, (3) at first consonant, then progress towards maximum tension at the ninth chord and then gradually return to consonance:

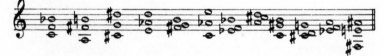

4. Proceed as in Question 3 but add the free part *above* the intervals given.

5. Repeat Question 3 but make the free part a succession of suspensions. In this way the free part will have to fulfil a satisfactory function in every two adjacent chords.

6. Add a free part (1) below and (2) above the following three-note chords so as to create good twelve-note harmony of relatively even tension throughout:

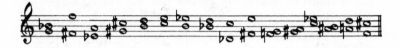

7. Continue the following *Capriccio* for violin and piano in a free twelve-note manner:

8. Write a composition for flute, vibraphone, and bass clarinet using a free twelve-note technique, beginning as follows:

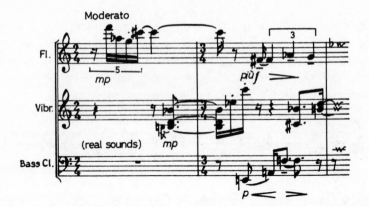

INDEX